LIFE AFTER DEATH

Rudolf Joseph Lorenz Steiner
February 27, 1861 – March 30, 1925

FROM THE WORKS OF DR. RUDOLF STEINER

LIFE AFTER DEATH

STEINER'S BOOK OF THE DEAD

Dr. Douglas J. Gabriel

Our Spirit, LLC
2023

OUR SPIRIT, LLC

P. O. Box 355

Northville, MI 48167
www.ourspirit.com
www.neoanthroposophy.com
www.gospelofsophia.com
www.eternalcurriculum.com

2023 Copyright © by Our Spirit, LLC

All rights reserved. No part of this publication may
Be reproduced, stored in a retrieval system, or transmitted,
in any form or by any means, electronic, mechanical,
recording, photocopying, or otherwise, without prior written
permission of the publisher.

ISBN: 979-8-9864415-5-9 (paperback)
ISBN: 979-8-9864415-6-6 (eBook)

Book Cover art by Charles Andrade at www.lazure.com

CONTENTS

Life After Death	1
Is There Life-After-Death?	2
The Background to Life Between Death and Rebirth	7
Sleep—Death's Little Sister	17
Steiner's Life Between Death and Rebirth	18
Kamaloka—a Place of Desire	22
Staying Connected with Loved Ones	29
Phases and Spheres Following Death	41
The Return to Another Birth	61
Theosophical Terms about the Afterlife	71
The Mysteries of Sleep and Dreams	83
Nightly Inspiration	89
The Materialistic Scientific View of Sleep and Dreams	95
Sleep and Dreams According to Rudolf Steiner	101
Selections from Rudolf Steiner's Works on Sleep	108
Rudolf Steiner on the Process of Sleep	
Michaelic Verse by Rudolf Steiner	195
Bibliography	197
About Dr. Rudolf Steiner	203

About the Author, Dr. Douglas Gabriel	205
Translator's Note	207

Life After Death

My anthroposophical teachers always recommended reading Rudolf Steiner's lectures, *Life Between Death and Rebirth* to those who had passed the threshold of death. This practice continued the loving connection between the reader and the person who has passed over the threshold. Generally, this practice went on for the first three days after the passing.

In a quiet and reverent mood, the reader transmits to the loved one the contents of the book which describes the realms the person will be traversing from death to another birth. These spiritual spheres that the person is traveling through need a road map to help understand the new atmosphere and the topology of the spiritual world. These spheres are the interpenetrating realms of hierarchical beings who inhabit these realms that are so beautifully described in the cosmology of spiritual science. They are often referred to as the realms of the "harmony of the spheres." Reading descriptions of these realms to the deceased helps them orient themselves in these spheres which they have been "born" into so recently.

The spiritual spheres have been referred to as a seven-storied mountain, Jacob's Ladder, the gradual path of awakening, the search for the Holy Grail, the steps of initiation, the stages of enlightenment, the Tibetan Seven Limb Practice, the mansions of heaven, and many other names. No matter what religion you may be, if you believe in the afterlife, you need to prepare for the spiritual world you will be "born" into through the process of death.

Most spiritual training in this life is done to prepare for what we will experience on the other side of the threshold, either through death, sleep, or the processes of initiation. The goal is to meet and communicate with the spiritual hierarchies, saints, and ascended beings who live in the spiritual world. It requires moral development and keen interest to learn the spiritual language that is being spoken in the realm of the spheres. It requires wakefulness, moral development, diligence, renunciation of the material world, preparation, concentration, contemplation, meditation and spiritual dialogue between the soul and spirit of the initiate to be awake in the spiritual world beyond the threshold of death. Spiritual training is a way to begin to see the eternal as it manifests in this world as a product of the unseen world.

Is There Life-After-Death?

Modern thinkers are often not aware of the path the individual eternal spirit travels between death and rebirth. This type of spiritual scientific training is rare in our day and the lack of awareness needs to be remedied on this side of the threshold, before death comes and it is too late to gain what is needed in the after-life. After death, the individual is not free to learn and love as they were in the Earth realm. Humans are individualized and seemingly "alone" in a body that has limitations and constrictions in the material world. This loneliness is the price we pay for personal freedom. We may accept or reject the gifts of the spiritual world from the unseen realms, the decision is ours.

It takes faith to develop the capacities to believe that there is a spiritual world or that there is life after death, let alone the belief in repeated human Earth incarnations, or what is generally called reincarnation. It takes a willingness to believe that human karma and reincarnation exist. The modern materialistic thinker has no proof that an after-life exists or that spiritual beings populate a realm where human beings can live after death.

Sleep is a little death, the sister of the after-life. Each night we go to a magical sleep realm that restores our physical body and refreshes us for a new day. Sleep is a little death followed by another birth into a material world that often feels as if it is not our home. Many might prefer to stay in the warm and comfortable realm of sleep, dreams, dreamless sleep, and night visions. The oppressive weight of the world is alleviated by the grace and mercy of sleep. The quiet darkness of the night is the mid-wife of our birth into the new day.

Immoral and guilty souls have trouble crossing into the realm of sleep as their own evil hounds them like the Furies of the Greeks. But the pure and noble soul uses sleep as a repast of refreshment, nourishment, and inspiration, often accompanied by intuitions upon waking in the morning that smooth the path ahead with pre-cognitive dreams, visions, and guidance. It seems that the realm of sleep is the 'great panacea' that heals all wounds for those moral souls who use it as an oasis of life.

The knowledge that the realm of sleep and death are the same is shocking to most modern thinkers. To find out that the "harmony of the spheres" is the interpenetrating music created by the Sun and the six planets that replicate themselves in our heart and major organs, comes as a revelation to most. The thought is simple; but the ramifications are awesome and cosmic. It is immediately understood by a sharp mind that if the realm of sleep and death are the same, and the realm of sleep is the cosmic healer, then it is a small step to understand that death is a temporary sleep wherein the human soul and spirit are healed and renewed for another day (incarnation) that continues to build upon the work of the last day (incarnation).

Rudolf Steiner pointed out that a healthy mind will automatically understand that reincarnation is a spiritual reality. Closely examining sleep will lead a clear thinker to the simple reality of reincarnation. Birth is followed by death, which is then followed by rebirth—and the cycle goes on.

Cognizing the great cosmic gifts and sacrifices that Christ has bestowed upon human evolution is the central task of wholesome spiritual development at our current stage of evolution. In light of this, it is imperative to realize that humans can only evolve spiritually while they are in the material world where freedom is obtained through suffering transformed into wisdom, and ultimately only finds fulfillment through love. Nonetheless, there are many that might assume that once we die we will immediately come to a complete understanding of the love of Christ; although Rudolf Steiner teaches us that one cannot come to fully understand the great mystery of the love of Christ upon first entering the realm of death. As this is only truly attainable through the Divine Grace that arises in response to our sincere strivings while dwelling within the realm of earthly life. Therefore, if they wish to truly evolve spiritually, each person must first strive through the path of freedom and love toward the Living Christ (the True Self) while still within the earthly realm.

Knowing Christ in this way leads ultimately to a knowledge of our own higher self, Spirit-Self (Manas) or Guardian Angel; which is a necessary stage of human spiritual development within the Consciousness Soul Period (5th Post-Atlantean Period; 1,414 AD-3,574 AD); whereby we transform the Consciousness Soul into the Spiritual Soul in preparation for receiving the Spirit-Self during the 6th Post-Atlantean Period (3,574 AD-5,734 AD). Which, of course, can occur earlier in those initiates that achieve future stages of development in advance of mankind.

In light of this, one must keep in mind that this is not merely a "religious" or "church oriented" view of Christ; for this is in reference to the higher self of all spiritually evolving people, and cannot be fully understood through everyday Christian doctrine or dogma. For knowing Christ in this way is the fruit of a direct experience of your higher self (Manas). Rudolf Steiner addresses some of these complexities in the volume *Nature and Spirit Beings: Their Effects in Our Visible World* (Stuttgart, February 8, 1908; GA 98):

> "…We must think of man as having brought with him his physical body, his etheric body and his astral body. Then three members develop: the sentient soul, the intellectual soul and

the consciousness soul, and finally Manas. The consciousness soul has its power from Jupiter, the intellectual soul from Mercury, the sentient soul from Mars and the Spirit-Self received its impulse from Venus."

This path of knowing is clarified further by Rudolf Steiner in a lecture entitled: *Esoteric Development and Supersensible Knowledge* (Vienna November 7, 1907; GA 98):

"…Self-knowledge is two-fold: first, it is the recognition of what the true self must do. Second, it is the knowledge of the higher self. But their knowledge is something quite different. You can read in the *Bible*: Adam knew his wife. [*Genesis 4*]—This is an expression for 'fertilization.' 'Know thyself' means: fertilize yourself with the wisdom inside of you, look at the soul as a feminine organ and fertilize yourself. If you want to gain self-knowledge, search inside of you, where you will be able to recognize all your mistakes. If you want to reach knowledge of the higher self, search outside of you; because there knowledge of the world is knowledge of the self. Everything is in the Sun because everything is Sun. We have to let go of ourselves. I have been told: 'You tell us about development and such things, but we want to achieve an uplifting of the soul, of the feelings.' One who speaks like that is his own enemy. Not by gawking into ourselves; but by learning to know the world in all its parts, bit by bit, will we become selfless and able to find self-knowledge and knowledge of God. There is no phrase worse than that one: 'One only has to look within oneself.'—There you will only find the lower self. One should search outside with love and one will discover."

Each human body is a temple that can be dedicated to Christ while dwelling within the material plane of existence. For if you align yourself with Christ during your waking hours you give Him the invitation to work further through healing transformative forces within the world of sleep.

> "Ask, and it shall be given you; seek, and ye shall find; knock, and it shall be opened unto you: For every one that asketh receiveth; and he that seeketh findeth; and to him that knocketh it shall be opened." *Matthew* (7:7-8)

Once your higher self (Spirit-Self/Manas/Sophia/Wisdom), has found a true awakening through Christ (Life-Spirit/Budhi/Logos/Love), then Christ can become the indwelling presence and ruler of your morally centered human heart, each person can then begin to learn the Language of the Spirit, a moral language that pervades the spiritual realms beyond the threshold.

> "And every man that hath this hope in him purifieth himself, even as he is pure."
> 1 *John* (3:3)

> "For where your treasure is, there will your heart be also."
> *Luke* (12:34)

> "Blessed are the pure in heart, for they shall see God."
> *Matthew* (5:8)

But this path must arise out of freedom; therefore, it is incumbent upon the striving aspirant of the spirit to take the first steps towards Christ in this earthly realm so that Christ might accompany the aspirant through the seven realms of the spiritual world, the mansions of heaven that Jesus Christ said he had gone ahead and prepared for each of us.

> "Then shall the King say unto them on his right hand, Come, ye blessed of my Father, inherit the kingdom prepared for you from the foundation of the world:" *Matthew* (25:34)

Learning about the mansions of heaven is the point of Steiner's lectures on the life between death and rebirth. Nowhere else in the Western esoteric tradition can you find a better description of life after death. What Steiner has done for us is to create a *"Western Book of the Dead"* based upon spiritual science. This new Steiner *"Western Book of the Dead"* is similar to the previous writings that were used to "cross the threshold", like the *Egyptian Book of the Dead* or the *Tibetan Book of the Dead*.

Rudolf Steiner's *Book of the Dead* is not only a book to study before you die; but rather, a book to be read to those who have died and passed over the threshold between the physical and spiritual worlds. It is with the comfort of this wisdom that the striving aspirant can consciously cross the threshold through spiritual practices at night through moral wakefulness, or at the moment of death. If this guidance is wed with the eternal wisdom that is gleaned from beholding the spirit as manifested in the material world, then the awakened aspirant can become a conscious and loving participant in the after-life world of the spirit.

The Background to Life Between Death and Rebirth

To understand the background to the series of lectures *Life Between Death and Rebirth*, it is helpful to look at what Rudolf Steiner's personal secretary, Dr. Guenther Wachsmuth, had to say about what was going on in Steiner's life at the time of the lectures. Wachsmuth gives us many details that illuminate the history of each lecture series and its place in Steiner's overall work. Wachsmuth's book *Life and Work of Rudolf Steiner*, is seen by many people as a completion of Steiner's unfinished autobiography *The Course of My Life*. We will draw from this book a selection that highlights the history behind *Life Between Death and Rebirth*.

Guenther Wachsmuth (October 4th, 1893-March 2nd, 1963) was a jurist, economist, member of the Executive Council of the Anthroposophic Society and leader of the Science Section at the Goetheanum, as well as Rudolf Steiner's personal secretary. It is thanks to his energetic coordinating activity that the second Goetheanum would open in 1928. Wachsmuth was a gifted student of Steiner who composed his richly detailed narrative of the culminating quarter century of Steiner's biography in *The Life and Work of Rudolf Steiner*.

The following extract is taken from: *The Life and Work of Rudolf Steiner, From the Turn of the Century to His Death*, by Guenther Wachsmuth and Translated by Olin D. Wannamaker & Reginald E. Raab, from Whittier Books, New York, 1955 (pages 181-185).

From Guenther Wachsmuth's,
The Life and Work of Rudolf Steiner

"In his lectures in Milan on October 26 and 27, 1912, Dr. Steiner developed the theme, prominent during the following months, *The Life of the Soul after Death*. On the journey to Austria, this was supplemented on November 3 by a lecture in Vienna on *The Latest Results of Occult Research Regarding Life Between Death and a New Birth* and he summarized this in a comprehensive course of lectures commencing on November 5 in Berlin under the title *Life Between Death and a New Birth in Relation to Cosmic Facts*.

The historical importance of this lecture cycle must be truly realized. Never before in the history of mankind had these questions been expounded in such a way as to include the details of actual events between death and reincarnation. In past centuries the existence of such a life had only been affirmed or denied in general. Rudolf Steiner had often, in the previous decade, referred to these facts as such and to certain aspects of that spiritual existence between a death and a new birth. But, just as in other realms of knowledge, he had displayed tireless patience as always in research while awaiting the hour when the fruits of his work could be presented as a higher unity.

The first experience Rudolf Steiner had of spiritual vision and conscious contact with the personalities of the dead occurred around 1868 when he was but seven years old; with his perception of the supersensible continually unfolding thereafter. This initial clairvoyant event occurred while he was living in the foothills of the eastern Austrian Alps in the village of Pottschach, where his father worked as a Telegraph operator for the Austrian Railways. On at least two occasions, once in a lecture in Berlin on February 4, 1913, Rudolf Steiner related the following story about when he saw an apparition of an aunt walk through a door, into the middle of the waiting room of the train station, where she made some odd gestures and said, "Try now, and in later life, to help me as much as you can," the apparition then vanished by drifting into the hearth. Elsewhere he related that although her death was completely unknown to him at the time, as she was living at a distant location; but unbeknownst to him she had tragically committed suicide around that same time. "My parents had no notice of her death. I sat in the waiting room of the train station and saw a vision of what had happened. I tried to tell my parents. They replied, 'Don't be a silly boy'. Some days later, I saw my father become pensive after receiving a letter. Later, in my absence he spoke with my mother, who cried for days thereafter. I heard the details of my aunt's death only years later." Thereafter, the critical response he received from his parents had taught him at a very early age to keep his supersensible experiences to himself.

In his autobiography, *The Course of My Life* (chapter 3) he refers especially to the year 1879, a period of life now thirty-three years in the past, to the fact that, during his philosophical and scientific studies, he had before him a spiritual vision of life after death:

> "I felt at that time duty bound to seek for the truth through philosophy. I had to study mathematics and natural science. I was convinced that I should find no relation with them unless I could place their findings upon a solid foundation of philosophy. But I beheld a spiritual world as reality. In perfectly clear vision the spiritual individuality of everyone was manifest to me. This had in the physical body and in action in the physical world merely its expression. It united itself with that which came as a physical germ from the parents. The dead human being I followed on his way into the spiritual world…"

What had been known and confirmed through so many years in spiritual vision, research, and constantly repeated experience, that for which he had systematically developed the foundations in knowledge, had now in its clarity and maturity to be placed in a comprehensive form before humanity as a treasure of knowledge and as help in the mastering of the problems of life. So, he said in the first lecture of the cycle referred to above, that in the year 1912 the moment had arrived for him to speak about these spiritual facts in a new manner "because just in the course of the summer and autumn the task confronted me of subjecting this realm to renewed spiritual research and of also setting forth a point of view which could not be touched upon earlier."

Since Rudolf Steiner very rarely interpolated allusions of so personal a kind in presenting the content of knowledge, this reference to the spiritual-karmic significance of recent months is of particular importance; for we have already referred to certain events coming to completion in the course of his life during these months. In light of this, it is important to understand that the manner in which the inner evolution of such a personality is so intimately connected with the karmic events unfolding in the earthly world that it reveals its own special karmic significance; for it is a unique point in the history of human evolution out of which this new approach to spiritual understanding became possible; and furthermore was considered by Rudolf Steiner to be a matter of duty, he characterized this as follows:

> "Only now is it possible to envision much of what exhibits to us the deep moral significance of the supersensible truths relevant to this realm. Besides all other prerequisites which have now only been hinted at, there is indeed another prerequisite—at least within our Movement—a prerequisite, one might say, which wounds the hearts of many persons in this proud and vain age of ours. Since one cannot permit oneself, however, to be deterred by such a consideration from the earnestness and truthfulness which we owe to our Movement, this prerequisite must continue to be held. This prerequisite consists in the fact that, in intimate and earnest work, really learning and devoting ourselves to the matter, we shall enter into what is obtained out of the spiritual worlds. We may affirm that for a number of years the relation of human beings on the physical plane to the spiritual world has changed from what it was, for example, during almost the whole of the nineteenth century.
>
> Until the last third of the nineteenth century, there was little access to the spiritual worlds. In proportion to the necessities in human evolution, very little content flowed into human souls out of the spiritual worlds. But now we

are living in an age in which the soul needs only to be receptive, needs only to surrender itself and to be prepared for the revelations out of the spiritual worlds to flow into it. And more and more receptive are certain individual souls becoming for whom, through the fact that they are conscious of the mission of their age, the streaming in of spiritual knowledge is a fact. An additional requirement, therefore, for spiritual science is that it shall not shut itself off from what can flow at the present time in any manner whatever out of the spiritual worlds into the souls."

The cosmic hour now rendered possible, and also demanded, an openness for what desired to enter into the consciousness of the human being; and, it has always been the task of the spiritual leader to arouse human beings in such a cosmic hour in order that at least some of them may confront the spiritual occurrence in wakefulness.

"The human being passes through the events of the spiritual world between death and a new birth in a very special manner. He experiences them, however, also upon Earth through initiation; he experiences them also—if he has prepared his soul—already even during existence in the physical body, in that he becomes in this way a participant in the spiritual worlds. One may assert, therefore, that what happens between death and a new birth and what is, indeed, a living through of the spiritual world,—this can be beheld through initiation."

One of the fundamental evolutionary truths of our age, to which Rudolf Steiner brought to the attention of mankind, was that in past epochs it might have sufficed at that time to merely believe in these things as an act of faith, and thereby find consolation in the belief that these truths would be unfolded in the after-death experience. He made clear that at this point in history a new stage in evolution had arrived for mankind and a supersensible reality was unfolding; whereby mankind should now become familiar with these forms of knowledge, not merely like vague expressions of dream-life but within the complete clarity of waking consciousness. This new development within the consciousness of modern humanity would become critically important as we move into the future; for spiritual and earthly events would gradually interpenetrate each other ever more intensively—thereby providing an awakening of the healing forces of the Holy Spirit if taken up with wonder, awe, and reverence as the proper mood of soul. On the other hand, if one does not bring about within their consciousness a harmonious synthesis of both the sensible and supersensible worlds while living on Earth, and thereby reject the supersensible through embracing a materialist worldview—disharmony or even illness could occur through the enactment of the unforgivable "sin against the Holy Spirit."

> "If we receive the witness of men, the witness of God is greater: for this is the witness of God which he hath testified of his Son. He that believeth on the Son of God hath the witness in himself: he that believeth not God hath made him a liar; because he believeth not the record that God gave of his Son. And this is the record, that God hath given to us eternal life, and this life is in his Son. He that hath the Son hath life; and he that hath not the Son of God hath not life." *1 John* (5:9-12)

In *The Life and Work of Rudolf Steiner: From the Turn of the Century to His Death*, Guenther Wachsmuth clearly characterizes the significance of this transition pointed out by Rudolf Steiner at the end of the 1912 lecture cycle *Life Between Death and a New Birth in Relation to Cosmic Facts:*

"…after having described the facts of spiritual existence, Dr. Steiner once more called attention to the inherent laws in spiritual research which led to these findings, and pointed out how at the beginning of the anthroposophical work his book *Theosophy* presented these phenomena rather in the psychic aspect, whereas now in the course of time the cosmographic aspect, so to speak—the position of the human soul in the great facts of cosmic evolution—could be added as an element of knowledge…"

"These are considerations which may show us how, within the presentation of the book *Theosophy*—only, in different words and in a different aspect there is already contained what has been described from a cosmic point of view, cosmographically as it were, during this winter. You have only to imagine that in one instance the subject is dealt with from the point of view of the soul, and in another from the point of view of the great cosmic relations, and you can reconcile the two descriptions and find a complete agreement, a complete parallelism. The conclusion I wish to draw from this is that you can see how far-reaching spiritual science is, and its methods must be such that, from all possible directions, there is brought together whatever can throw light on the Spirit world. Even though something is added years later to what has been said in previous years, there need be no contradiction, for these things are not derived from philosophic systems or human speculation, but from spiritual research."

"Together with the content of research, the path and the method were always set forth by Rudolf Steiner which led to these findings, and we are consequently able not only to receive a new world picture but to share in the experience of its genesis and development…"

"…Thus, the spiritual world, since the beginning of the twentieth century, bestows upon man the knowledge of his supersensible spheres of existence; it extends the view for him beyond birth and death and unveils for him the laws of evolution in future development. He may accept or reject this, but he has been given a free choice between inner healing and strengthening on the one hand and lethargy and pessimism on the other."

"The threshold can be crossed by man and the responsibility is handed over to him in accordance with his stage of maturity. The cosmic age has entrusted him alike with a new burden and a new dignity, and the development of the present century will show whether the question addressed to him will find its answer."

Sleep—
'Death's Little Sister'

As an introduction to forming a living Imagination of the heavenly spheres that a person traverses after death, Rudolf Steiner's remarks on sleep are most instructive. Sleep is 'death's little sister' and is a small taste of what happens to the soul after death. Each night, the soul and spirit rise-up from the etheric and physical bodies. The ego (I Am) and the soul traverse the realms of Moon, Venus, Mercury, and the Sun. For those whose consciousness is developed enough to stay "awake" in these realms; the dreams, visons and the heavenly 'harmonies of the spheres' can inspire the soul with spiritual strength, courage, and love. The realms of sleep and the after-life are the same interpenetrating planetary spheres that are inscribed by the Sun and the six major planets. Understanding the spheres of the unseen world through sleep can help prepare for the journey through those same spheres after death.

On numerous occasions Rudolf Steiner gave us beautiful and comprehensive living Imaginations of the realm of sleep and the planetary spheres we transverse with our soul and spirit each night. In London April 24, 1922, printed as the first lecture of *Planetary Spheres and Their Influence on Mans Life on Earth and in the Spiritual Worlds, I. The Threefold Sun and the Risen Christ*, Rudolf Steiner gives a most profound indication about the critical importance of understanding the realms of soul and spirit that the human being lives in while on Earth in both sleep and after death.

"It is of the first importance that there should be in this present time a certain number of people who know where man stands in his spiritual evolution and know also what must be his next step if civilization is not to go completely under. For what is happening today? In speaking to you, my dear friends, I can use anthroposophical terminology and say at once that the Ahrimanic forces, which are at work wherever man thinks or acts on a materialistic basis, are in our day trying to chain man to the Earth by gaining possession of his intellect. They are at this moment very powerful, these Ahrimanic forces, and they are searching out all kinds of ways to get access to the souls of men, with the object of enticing them to the adoption of a purely materialistic outlook, a purely intellectual understanding of the world. It is on this account important that there should be, as I said, a certain number of persons who know how the evolution of man has to proceed in order for him to reach his goal."

Steiner's *Life Between Death and Rebirth*

The selections below are taken from: *Life Between Death and Rebirth, The active connection between the living and the dead*, Sixteen Lectures, Rudolf Steiner, Anthroposophic Press, New York, 1968. (Translated by René M. Querido, GA 140)

The sixteen lectures compiled in this volume were given by Rudolf Steiner in different European cities throughout the years 1912 and 1913. They deal with the experiences of the human soul during and after death. He describes the states of consciousness experienced by our deceased loved ones and how we, taking into account their new consciousness, can communicate with them and even help them. While reading these descriptions, it becomes clear that excarnated souls need the spiritual support of those presently incarnated, and that those still on Earth in turn derive enlightenment and support from their former Earth companions.

Man's Life on Earth and in the Spiritual Worlds,
by Rudolf Steiner

"Just as here on Earth we are connected with the plants, with the minerals, with air, so are we connected in the night with the movements of the planets, and with the constellations of the fixed stars. From the moment we fall asleep, the starry heavens become our world, even as the Earth is our world when we are awake.

"Coming now to describe rather more in detail how we take our way after falling asleep, we find we can distinguish different spheres through which we pass. First comes the sphere where the I and the astral body—that is to say, the soul of man as it finds itself in sleep—feel united with the movements of the World of the planets. When we wake up in the morning and slip into our physical body, we have in us, as we know, our lungs, our heart, our liver, our brain. In the first sphere with which we come in contact after falling asleep—and it will also be again the last sphere we enter before awaking—we have in us the forces of the movements of the planets.

"This does not mean of course that we receive into us every night the entire planetary movements; we carry within us a little picture, as it were, wherein the movements of the planets are reproduced. And this picture is different for each single human being. That, then, is the first experience every one of us encounters after falling asleep. We follow, as it were, with our astral body all that happens with the planets, as they move out there in the wide spaces of the Universe; we experience it all in our astral body in a sort of planetary globe.

"Very soon after you have fallen asleep, the heart-eye begins also to look back at what has been left lying in bed. Your ego and astral body look back with the heart-eye upon your physical and etheric bodies. And the picture of planetary movements that you are now experiencing in your astral body, rays back to you from your etheric body; you behold a reflection of it in your etheric body.

"Here it is that the Christ appears before us as a spiritual Sun and becomes our guide; and then all the confusion resolves itself into a kind of harmony that we hear and understand. That this should be so, that we should have in the time of sleep the Christ for our guide, is a matter of the very greatest importance for us. For, the moment we enter this sphere and begin to have all around us the living interplay of constellations of the Zodiac and movements of the planets—at this moment we encounter also our karma. With our Sun-eye we behold our karma. Yes, it is indeed so, every human being has sight of his karma—in sleep. All that is left of the perception in waking life, is a kind of faint echo vibrating in the feelings.

"Such then is the experience man undergoes every night between falling asleep and awaking,—an experience he owes to the fact that his soul and spirit have kinship with the Cosmos. For, even as he is related to the Earth with his physical and etheric bodies, so with his soul and spirit, with his astral body and ego, is man related to the Cosmos. And when he has come away from his physical and etheric bodies and has grown out into the cosmic world, and the experiences he undergoes there shine back to him, in a kind of inner picture, from the part of him that remains in bed, he feels very deeply connected with the Cosmos and would, in fact, be strongly drawn to go still further out, to go out beyond the Zodiac,—were it not for the presence of another force that draws him back.

"All other forces—the forces of the planets and of the fixed stars—tend to draw us out into the distant Cosmos, the Moon wants to place us once more into the world of men. The Moon draws us away from the Cosmos. The Moon has forces that are directly opposed to the forces both of Sun and of stars; it ensures for us our kinship with the Earth. It is accordingly the Moon that brings us back every night,—drawing us away from the Zodiac experiences into the experiences of the planets, and thence into the experiences of Earth, taking us back once again into our physical body.

"When man goes to sleep, he remains still in close connection with the forces of the Moon. The forces of the Moon point out to him every night afresh the significance of his life on Earth. This is made possible by the fact that he can see in his etheric body the reflection of all his experiences of the night. At death, however, man withdraws his etheric body from the physical body. Then begins, as you know, the memory that looks back over the last Earth life. The etheric body expands and fills for a few days a cosmic cloud.

"Every night we live our way as cloud, as mist, into the 'Mist of the Worlds.' In the night, this cloud of mist which we are, is there without the ether-body; but when we die, our etheric body is present with it for the first few days. Then the etheric body gradually dissolves away into the Cosmos, memory fades and disappears, and we have—instead of a reflection of star experiences thrown back from the part of us we left lying in bed—we have now, after death, an immediate inner experience of the movements of the planets and of the constellations of the fixed stars.

"Man has however, even after death, something left in him of the force which he inherits from the Moon, enough to enable him to remain for a season in the soul world, with gaze still fixed upon the Earth. Then, he passes on to Spirit-Land and here he feels and knows that he is undergoing an experience where he is beyond the zodiac, beyond the heavens and the fixed stars. Such is the course of man's life in the time between death and new birth."

Kamaloka—a Place of Desire

The first stage that a person goes through after death is called in Sanskrit, 'Kamaloka' ("place of desire"), that realm where desire and passion binds a soul to earthly vices until the attachment dissolves and frees the soul from its addictions and uncontrolled astral impulses. Steiner describes the after-death state very succinct terms in Lecture VI of his lecture series entitled, *Planetary Spheres and Their Influence on Man's Life on Earth and in the Spiritual Worlds.* We present a selection from that lecture which describes in detail the nature of Kamaloka. In his lectures *Life Between Birth and Death*, there is a description of Kamaloka that needs further indications to understand this realm more fully. We offer the selections below as a more detailed picture of the stage after death called Kamaloka and offer it here before the selections from *Life Between Death and Rebirth.*

Life Between Death and Rebirth, **by Rudolf Steiner**

"You are already aware what awaits the human being immediately after death. His physical body being laid aside, within and about him he has his I, his astral body and his etheric body. From birth till death, as you know, the etheric body remains united with the physical body. Even in sleep, it is only with the I and astral body that the human being is outside the physical,—and thus outside the etheric body too. Then for a short while after death (only a matter of days), man still inhabits his etheric body—his body of formative forces—and he is thereby enabled to look back on the whole course of his past earthly life, which is in fact always contained in the etheric body.

"Yet, it is not for long that we can retain the etheric body after death. Belonging as it does to the entire Cosmos, the etheric body is always wanting to expand. Only the physical body, in which it stays throughout our life, holds it together. And then, when the physical body's coherent power is no longer ours, straightway the etheric body begins to expand, so much so that in a few days' time it is there for us no longer. It is as when you take a little drop of water; the drop is there before you; warm it and it evaporates and expands in all directions; then it is there no more—you can no longer see it. So does the ether-body expand into the Cosmos after death; after a very few days it is there no more.

"Yet at the same time, we see glistening and shining forth in our etheric body a reflection of the great universe. The entire starry heavens are there in the etheric body. Indeed, you cannot ever see the etheric body apart from the physical without its showing you at once the starry world on every hand—the planets and the fixed stars too. It is the planets and the fixed stars which at long last receive our etheric body. Initiation-science shows that we can hold the pictures in our etheric body only for three or four days at the most; then they vanish, and to avoid being disconnected altogether we must return into our physical body before this happens, otherwise the etheric body will no longer hold together. And thus indeed, a few days after death the etheric body vanishes, we have it no longer. Yet we ourselves are thereby progressively received into the world of stars.

"At first, when divested of our etheric body, we feel like strangers amid the world of stars. Only the Moon, only the lunar forces seem, as it were, familiar to us there. The Moon emerges on the one hand as in an after-image of its physical appearance. Yet at the same time we now begin to discover what kind of spiritual forces are connected with it. For the soul who has passed through the gate of death, the Moon is transformed, as it were, into a colony of spiritual Beings, and Jahve is their leader. Yes, it is through the Moon—through the Jahve powers—that we learn the significance of death.

"Through his ethereal and subsequent astral experiences, the man himself goes on into the spiritual world, yet something of importance happens also here on Earth. From the physical body a spiritual apparition is released, emerging, as it were, out of the human body. While the real human being goes upon his way, here on the other hand, we might say, another being issues from the human body.

"Truly it is so when a human being dies. There lies his physical body as the man himself is departing from it, and simultaneously another being leaves it. What is this other being? It is the forces of the Moon, living as they do also here on Earth. Concentrated though they be in the cosmic entity we call the Moon, the range of these forces extends far and wide, and on the Earth they are made manifest in the powers of death. Moreover, the powers of death are at the same time those of birth. They lead the human being into Earthly life and are made manifest when he leaves it. We thus begin to realize the deep connection between birth and death.

"Take all the human beings who die in successive times. From each of them in turn the apparition of death, as it were, comes forth and joins a spiritual atmosphere which is there around the Earth no less than is the air we breathe. This spiritual atmosphere contains what death gives up and birth receives. From the very forces that soar upward, as it were, from human corpses, human beings in their turn, are born. Spiritually, our powers of growth are intimately connected with this sphere of death-force—or forces made manifest in death—which surrounds the Earth.

"These spiritual forces—at once of death and birth, as we have seen—are forces of the Moon, and into them is mingled all that the dead human being, all along the way from birth till death, accumulated by way of moral powers, moral values. Have you been good in any way,—in the sphere of these death-Moon-forces you will find, as it were, a specific being, imbued with inner force deriving from your goodness. Yet the same being is imbued with all that derives from your badness. It is a being we ourselves engender, all the time, while living on the Earth. Unaware of it as we are in our normal consciousness, we bear it in us. We leave it every night when we are sleeping, for in effect this entity remains in the physical body when we go out of it in sleep. There also is left behind this real being which we ourselves give birth to during Earthly life—the bearer of our karma.

"This being now remains with us after death so long as we are in the realm of the Moon forces. Indeed, just because this being keeps us amid the Moon-forces, that is, in the near neighborhood of Earth, during the first period after death we are obliged to remain connected with these lunar forces and with our own karma, so much so that we live again through all the deeds we did on Earth from birth till death. We have to live them through again in a spiritual form of being, three times as fast as we did on Earth. We live them through again in backward order. So do we spend a period of time after death, obliged to do things intimately connected with our Earthly deeds. We are united, it is true, no longer through the physical body with the Moon-forces of death (for we have laid the physical body aside), and yet as beings of soul and spirit we are obliged to carry out deeds intimately connected with our deeds on Earth. And as we thus go through our life again in backward order, our karma is ever more convincingly brought home to us.

"If I have been responsible for any deed which makes me appear a morally imperfect man, and if I were not to go through it all again deeply and inwardly as I am doing now, I should not feel the strong impulse to make it good. I should not want to free myself from my failing. Precisely by experiencing the deed all over again in soul and spirit, the urge is born in me to overcome it by a better action. Not for anything in the world would the dead forgo this opportunity to make 'good again', for this alone will give him power to achieve his full humanity,—will give him strength to be made whole. In this respect you may be sure, even as a landscape looks very different seen from the valley or from a mountain-top, life itself looks different seen from this physical world where we are now and from yonder side. Only too often the relationships of Earthly life to the life after death, which after all transcends the physical, are misjudged for this reason."

Note:

† Jahve is their leader:

> Jahve or Jehovah is the singular name for the 'Ĕlōah or Spirit of Form [1] of the Moon that separated the Moon from the Earth in the Lemurian Epoch beginning the separation of the sexes; as told in the Garden of Eden story about Adam and Eve in *The Book of Genesis*. Furthermore, it was Jehovah that Christ worked through in the story of Moses regarding the "burning bush" and the "pillar of a cloud" and "pillar of fire." [2]
>
>> [1] Spirits of Form, Greek: Exousíai, ἐξουσίαι; Latin: Potestates; English: Powers, Authorities; Hebrew: 'Ĕlōhīm, "God(s), Heavenly Power(s)."
>>
>> [2] "And when forty years were expired, there appeared to him in the wilderness of mount Sina an angel of the

Lord in a flame of fire in a bush. When Moses saw it, he wondered at the sight: and as he drew near to behold it, the voice of the Lord came unto him, Saying, I am the God of thy fathers, the God of Abraham, and the God of Isaac, and the God of Jacob." *Acts* (7:30-32)

"And the LORD went before them by day in a pillar of a cloud, to lead them the way; and by night in a pillar of fire, to give them light; to go by day and night: He took not away the pillar of the cloud by day, nor the pillar of fire by night, from before the people." *Exodus* (13:21-22)

Staying Connected with Loved Ones

Death is not the end of the road; it is a new beginning to a relationship with our loved ones that is certainly changed but not ended. You may follow a loved one who, has passed over the threshold of death, through the spheres Dr. Steiner describes in such beautiful Moral Imaginations, and calculate an approximate timeline of what they are doing year after year. As you remember your interactions with your loved one, who is experiencing the backward Kamaloka experience themselves in a triple-speed playback of their lives, you can align your prayers and communications with the loved one in an appropriate, synchronized manner. You can actually participate in what they are experiencing.

For example, a loved one, who has passed away, experiences the effects she had on the world around her as she reviews her life in a backwards fashion. If you spent years in a close relationship with her before she passed over the threshold, then she will be experiencing everything she did to you and with you; but, from the perspective of the karma it created with you. What she sowed, she will reap in the spheres after death. She can no longer sow new karma until she incarnates into a new physical body in the material world. She is now experiencing the "effects of her life's willpower and deeds."

The dead experience their effects upon the outer world and the people they encountered. If they were good and kind, then they get good and kind returns through karma. Therefore, you can actively participate in their karmic review by rejoicing in the good and offering forgiveness, mercy, and love for the bad in a way that is aligned with the actual timing they are going through in their life review.

For instance, one year after a loved one's passing you can realize that she is in her life review of what happened three years ago (triple speed playback review). You can concentrate on that time and meditate on what transpired between the two of you. If it was an argument, you can forgive and heal the wound in yourself, even though she cannot change the past circumstances, you can. This is true because of the fact that you still have free will and can carry out an action in the physical world; you can in reality, change the karmic impact of the past deed in yourself and thus affect her at the same time through balancing karma. She no longer has free will and cannot create new karma while going through the life review passing through the various spheres. Thus, she is subject to experiencing the karma she created; but you, being on this side of threshold, can change your karmic reaction to the negative karma of the three-year-old argument and help transform it in yourself and subsequently turn the past deed into something good for the both of you. You have the amazing ability to help the Lord of Karma, Christ, mitigate her karmic load.

In the Roman Catholic faith this type of karmic mitigation is called praying for those in Purgatory. The faithful, on this side of the threshold, pray for those who have sins to pay for in Purgatory and because of the prayers of the faithful, the deceased person's time in Purgatory is shortened. This is some type of karmic mitigation, power of love, and after-death forgiveness given through the mercy of the Lord of Karma. Love, even after death, has the power to open the gates of Purgatory, and perhaps even Hell itself.

Life Between Death and Rebirth, by Rudolf Steiner

"The first period after death is such that we can only establish a good connection with souls who have remained on the Earth or with those who have died about the same time as ourselves. Here, the closest connections continue to be effective beyond death. Much can be done by the so-called living who have remained on the Earth. Because one has a connection with the departed soul, he can inform him of his own knowledge of the spiritual world acquired on the Earth. This is possible above all by reading to the dead.

"We can perform the greatest service to a person who has died by forming a picture of that person in our soul and softly reading a work of spiritual science to him, instructing him as it were. We can also convey to the departed the thoughts we have made our own, always vividly picturing the one who has passed on as we do so. We should be generous in this respect. This enables us to bridge the abyss that separates us from the dead. It is not only in extreme cases that we can help the dead in this way. No, it is true in every case. It provides a comforting feeling that can alleviate the sorrow that is experienced when a person whom one has loved passes on.

'The outcome of reading to the dead has proved itself to be particularly beautiful. It has shown itself to be a special service and one of the greatest deeds of love that can be performed."

The Path to the Spheres

"The first condition necessary for ascending into the spiritual world and for understanding the experiences gained in that realm is complete inner rest and steadiness of soul. All anxiety, all excitement and worry must cease in order to obtain inner calmness. During the time that we wish to lift ourselves into higher worlds, all interests in outer life must be extinguished.

"One learns to know the period between death and rebirth either by initiation or by going through the portal of death. In the super-sensible world, we must allow things to approach us for everything is reversed in the spiritual world. We must develop inner silence and then things will come to us.

"As we approach initiation, our soul undergoes the same experiences as those during the period between death and a new birth. But just as on Earth we receive our perceptions by means of the senses, so after death we receive them by way of visions. The world of visions presents at first only a reflection of ourselves. The whole of our life after death consists of visions that are mirror-images of reality. Just as we perceive the physical world by means of colors that the eye conjures forth for us, and sounds mediated by the ear, we experience the spiritual world after death by means of visions in which we are enveloped.

"Beings of the Hierarchies are working on the visions that surround us; they shine upon this mist as the Sun's rays irradiate the clouds. They surround us like a cloud and on the basis of them we must develop the faculty to receive the light of the hierarchies. It is therefore of the utmost importance that we cross the threshold of death with moral strength that will keep our soul open to the light of the hierarchies.

"There is no greater fear after death than darkening of consciousness. It is simply an unquestionable fact that souls deficient in religious thoughts experience a dimming of consciousness as a result of this deficiency. Shortly after death the consciousness of a materialist is dimmed, even extinguished.

"To the eyes of the spirit, it is disclosed that the human being on the Earth between birth and death, contracted as he is into the smallest possible space, emerges from it when he lays aside his physical body and expands farther and farther out into the universe. Having passed through the gate of death, he grows stage by stage out into the planetary spheres. First of all, he expands as far as the area marked by the orbit of the Moon;

the sphere indicated by the position of the Moon then becomes his outermost boundary. When that point has been reached, Kamaloka is at an end.

"Continuing to expand, he grows into the sphere formed by the orbit of Venus, later the orbit of Mercury. Then as his magnitude increases, his outermost boundary is marked by the apparent course of the Sun. Thus, as the human being ascends into the spiritual worlds he expands into the planetary system, first into the sphere of the Moon, and ultimately into the outermost sphere, that of Saturn. All this is necessary in order that he shall come into contact with those forces needed for his astral body, which can be received only from the planetary system.

"A soul with a moral disposition, a soul whose ideas are the outcome of purified will, becomes a sociable spirit and invariably finds the bridges and connections with the spiritual beings in whose sphere he is living. Whether we are isolated or sociable spirits is determined by our moral or immoral disposition of soul.

"Spiritual science shows that during life between death and rebirth the human being encounters certain other beings. Just as here he meets the many beings of the various kingdoms of nature, so after death he meets the beings of higher hierarchies and certain elemental beings. If a person goes through life without any sense of judgment, this is due to the fact that between death and rebirth he was unable to meet those beings who could have given him the appropriate forces to enable him to be morally and intellectually effective in this life. But the possibility and the ability to meet certain beings between death and rebirth depends on the last life.

"If during Earthly life we do not occupy ourselves with thoughts relating to the super-sensible, if during our life we have been completely immersed in the external sense world, if we only lived in our intellect inasmuch as it was directed to the physical world, then we make it impossible for ourselves between death and a new birth to encounter certain beings and to receive abilities from them for a subsequent life. The realm beyond remains dim and dark for us, and we are unable to find the forces of higher hierarchies in the darkness. Man then, between death and a new birth, passes by those beings from whom he should receive forces for his next Earthly life.

"The beings are there, and we can only reach them providing we have kindled the light in our last Earthly life by means of our interest in the spiritual world. After death, we are unable to penetrate the darkness unless we have taken the light with us through the gate of death. The light for the life beyond must be carried upward from the Earth."

Traveling Through the Cosmic Realms

"We travel through the cosmic universe after death through seven realms. To begin with, we go through the planets of our planetary system. We experience a Moon period, a Venus period, a Mercury period, a Sun period, a Mars period, a Jupiter period, and a Saturn period. Following these we go into the surroundings of our planetary system and then later commence our return journey. Now we encounter those forces and the beings from whom we must receive what we need to build up our next Earthly life.

"When we cross the gate of death we are, to begin with, occupied with the remains, the memories and the connections of our last Earthly embodiment. For a period of decades during the first stages after death, an individual looks back in retrospect in a sense on his last incarnation. He is still involved with what remains in the astral body as forces from the last Earthly life but increasingly he enters into the sphere of the planets and the Cosmos. He gradually enters a realm where he comes into contact with the beings of the higher hierarchies. Man must encounter these beings because this enables him to gather the forces he needs when later on, through birth, he again enters physical existence.

"The human soul can journey through the realm between death and a new birth in a twofold way. It is possible for the soul to wander through the realm of the higher hierarchies as if stumbling in the darkness without being able to receive the corresponding gifts from the higher hierarchies because of inner tendencies. In order to receive the gifts from the higher hierarchies between death and rebirth, one must be able to behold and confront these beings consciously. Pictorially speaking, one can wander in darkness, without light (spiritual light) through this realm, through the experiences one should have in the presence of the beings of the higher hierarchies.

"The interaction with the hierarchies can also be accomplished in such a way that, according to the necessities of our karma, their gifts to us are illuminated so that we receive them in the right manner. This light can shine forth only from ourselves—the light that enables us to pass the beings of the higher hierarchies so that they can rightly hand their gifts to us, so that we do not fail to grasp what we should receive.

"Souls who have unfolded only few feelings and sentiments transcending the affairs of Earthly life remain bound to the Earth sphere by their own cravings for a considerable time. Even outwardly it is easy to understand that a person who for a whole lifetime has cultivated only such feelings as can be satisfied by means of bodily organs and Earthly conditions can but remain bound to the Earth sphere for a certain time.

"What is experienced after death is that one is emerging from the body and one's whole soul-being is expanding. The human being grows, in a spiritual sense, to gigantic dimensions. He grows out into the spheres. The spheres of the dead are not separate from each other but are spatially intermingled. A sense of separateness arises because consciousness is separate. Beings may be completely intermingled without knowing anything of one another.

"First it must be emphasized that as the person expands into other spheres, all his imperfections are there inscribed. He expands from the Moon sphere into the Venus sphere and something is inscribed by him in all the spheres, in the Mercury sphere, the Sun sphere, the Mars sphere, the Jupiter sphere, the Saturn sphere and even beyond.

"Thus, after having cast away more or less completely what still draws him to the Earth, the human being journeys through the planetary spheres and even beyond them. The contact thus established with the corresponding forces provides what he needs in his evolution between death and a new birth. He comes into contact with the higher hierarchies and receives the gifts they bestow. When the expansion has been completed, he contracts again until he has become minute enough to unite as a spirit-seed with what comes from the parents.

"This is indeed a wonderful mystery. When the human being passes through the gate of death, he himself becomes an ever-expanding sphere. His potentialities of soul and spirit expand. He becomes a gigantic being and then again contracts. What we have within us has in fact contracted from the planetary universe. Quite literally we bear within us what we have lived through in a planetary world.

"Between death and rebirth our perfections and imperfections are faithfully recorded in the Akasha Chronicle. Certain attributes are inscribed in the Moon sphere, others in the Venus sphere, others in the Mercury sphere, others in the Mars sphere, others in the Jupiter sphere, and others in the Saturn sphere. When we are returning to an incarnation in a physical body and our being is slowly contracting, we encounter everything that was inscribed on the outward journey. In this way our karma is prepared. On the path of return we can inscribe into our own being the record of an imperfection we ourselves first inscribed into the Akasha Chronicle. Then we arrive on the Earth. Because there is within us everything we inscribed into our being on the return journey, our karma unfolds. Up above, however, everything still remains inscribed.

"These inscriptions that remain in the heavenly spheres work together in a remarkable way. They are engraved into the spheres, into the Moon sphere, Venus sphere, and so on. These spheres are involved in certain movements so that the following may happen. Let us say that a person has inscribed one of his imperfections into the Moon sphere. While passing through the Mars sphere he has inscribed there a quality of his character through the fact that he acquired in that sphere a certain element of aggressiveness that was not previously in him. Now on the return journey he passes through the Mars sphere again and comes back to the Earth. He lives on the Earth and has received into his karma what he has inscribed in the Mars sphere but at the same time it stands recorded above him. Up there is Mars, in a certain relationship to the Moon. Because Mars stands in a certain relationship to the Moon, the inscription of the aggressive element and the person's imperfections are, as it were, in the same constellation.

"The consequence is that when the one planet stands behind the other, they work in conjunction. This is the time when the individual in question will tackle his imperfections with the aggressive quality acquired from Mars. The position of the planets really does indicate what the man himself has first inscribed into these spheres.

"So, it is really the moral inheritance deposited by us between death and rebirth that appears again in a new life as a stellar constellation in our karma. That is the deeper basis of the connection between the stellar constellation and man's karma. During the life of a person between death and a new birth we perceive how significantly he is connected with the whole Cosmos."

The Akasha Chronicle

"What is inscribed in the Akasha Chronicle between the Earth and the Moon is of special importance because it is there that imperfections are recorded. The inscribing of these imperfections is governed by the view that every record there is of significance for the individual's own evolution, either furthering or hindering his progress. Because it is there inscribed in the Akasha Chronicle between Earth and Moon, it also becomes significant for the evolution of the Earth as a whole.

"When human souls go through the Gate of Death, they enter a realm where the connection with life on Earth is maintained by the recollection of what has happened there. For a long period after death man re-experiences what has happened on Earth and has to rid himself of the longing for his physical body. During this time, he learns to live as a soul-spirit being. One sees one's own inner life that has run its course in thoughts, in mental representations. One recalls the relationships one has had with his fellow men.

"If one seeks to look down upon it, the Earth offers a special aspect. One has the urge to look down. The urge to remember the Earth accompanies one throughout the whole of life between death and a new birth. As long as man is called to journey from life to life, the consciousness remains that he is destined for the Earth, that he must return again and again to the Earth if he would develop himself rightly. We can see this with the dead because if he were to lose completely the thoughts that link him to the Earth, he would also lose the thought of his own ego. Then, he would no longer be aware that he "is", and this would result in the most dreadful feeling of anguish. Man must not lose his connection with the Earth.

"It is important for the dead that those with whom they were connected on Earth carry every evening thoughts of the spiritual world with them into sleep. The more thoughts about the spiritual world we carry with us into sleep, the greater the service we perform for those we have known on Earth who have died before us. One who died and has no one on Earth who carries spiritual thoughts with him in sleep is famished and may be compared to one banished to a barren island on Earth. The dead person who cannot find a soul in whom spiritual feelings dwell experiences himself as if in a desert void of everything that is needed to sustain life. Such insight should lead to the practice, proven to be effective by many of our friends, that I would like to term, the 'reading to the dead.' To read to the dead is of untold significance.

"Now it is literally true that man, when he has crossed the portal of death, lives in that super-sensible world in which there is no death. He can enter these realms, but he cannot annihilate himself because he is received into worlds where there can be no destruction. There is something of a similar nature to death in the super-sensible world, yet it is quite different from death as we know it. One would have to call it in human language, loneliness. Death can never mean the annihilation of something that takes place in the super-sensible worlds; but, loneliness does arise. Loneliness in the super-sensible world is comparable to death here. It is not destruction—but it is far more intense than loneliness as we know it on Earth. It takes the form of looking back upon one's own being. One only knows what this fully means when it happens, that is, to know nothing except to know about oneself.

"After death, we expand in such a way that we become the Moon, just as on Earth we are our brain. We expand into Saturn so that we become Saturn, just as we are now our spleen. Man becomes a macrocosmic being. When the soul has departed from the body, it expands into the entirety of the planetary system so that all souls simultaneously dwell within the same spatial area.

"The deeper we enter into the super-sensible world, the less do particular relationships obtain. We still find individual relationships in the astral world; but, the higher we ascend, the more we find that what weaves between separate beings no longer continues. Now, there are beings everywhere. The relationships among them are of a soul nature. We need these also in order not to be lonely. It is the mission of the Earth that we make contacts from person to person because otherwise we remain solitary in the spiritual world."

Phases and Spheres Following Death

Each sphere we enter after death is another rung on the ladder to the seven heavens, another level on the 'seven story mountain', another way-station to our 'mansion' in our Father's kingdom. Our personal life, our family, our nation, our beliefs, and our relationship to the world are all inscribed into the Akasha Chronicle on this side of the threshold, and then is, more or less, "read back to us" after we die; much like the stories of the "Book of Life" found in most spiritual traditions. Everything we experience as karmic debt after death is something we created as a hindrance to directly experiencing the Holy Trinity and the Spiritual Hierarchies in all their glory and majesty while we lived on Earth, in the physical world. If we are blind to the spirit, it is because we have chosen to be. We really do reap what we sow. This is why so many naïve people speculate that we finally get to know the "truth" of life only after death, when the "truth" is revealed to us, when our karma is shown to us.

Spiritual scientific knowledge not only prepares the aspirant for what is to come in the future by providing the mind with a comprehensive cosmology; but, it also informs intellectual clairvoyance through the ability to act outside of time and space. As we learn about the spiritual spheres that we "live in" during sleep and after death, we find that as an aspirant on the road to initiation we can directly work in those realms of sleep and death through meditation, prayer, and communion with the divine. Divine spiritual beings live in those realms, and we can communicate with them in our own time through clear, wakeful consciousness, not just through dreams, dreamless sleep, or trance states of consciousness. Learning about those spiritual realms prepares the aspirant for crossing consciously into those worlds and develops the supersensible organs of perception that can perceive the beings in the spiritual world and learn the Language of the Spirit which is spoken there. This is the same language we use to speak with the dead and with which we can listen to what they have to teach us.

We are tremendously fortunate to have the spiritual scientific view of life after death and life in the spiritual world during sleep (and conscious initiation) as presented by Rudolf Steiner. Nowhere else does any spiritual teacher define, describe, and characterize what these realms of the spiritual world look like or the many ways of their mysterious nature. That is why Dr. Steiner's research is so important for the aspirant in today's world of literally a smorgasbord of spiritual offerings. Spiritual research, like Steiner's, should be able to be "put into practice" and gain results, or it is another useless millstone around the neck of the seeker. If spiritual realms exist, then the spiritual teacher should be able to tell the student how to get there in a tried-and-true fashion. Thus, studying Dr. Steiner's "book of the dead" can produce immediate and direct results for both those alive and those who have crossed the threshold.

Let us continue to examine what Dr. Steiner tells us about those spiritual spheres that we can visit consciously through his explicit descriptions of life between death and rebirth.

Life Between Death and Rebirth, by Rudolf Steiner

"For the first phases after death, our world consists of the relationships, the friendships that we formed with fellow human beings on Earth, and that now continues. For instance, if the matter is investigated with super-sensible perception, one finds the departed souls in the vicinity of a person whom it can follow on Earth. Many people in our time live with those who have died recently or at some earlier period. One also sees how many come together with a number of their ancestors to whom they were related by blood. The seer often comes upon the fact that the departed soul links itself to ancestors that have died centuries ago, but this only lasts for a certain period of time. The person would again feel exceedingly lonely if other connections did not exist which, though far off, yet prepare the person to be sociable in the spiritual world.

"A phase approaches when souls who have gone through the gate of death without any moral soul qualities feel very lonely. People who are endowed with a moral soul disposition are simply of greater value here than people lacking in morality. Between death and rebirth people also group themselves according to the moral concepts and soul dispositions they have in common.

"This is followed by a phase of development that even those who are endowed with a moral disposition of soul feel lonely if they lack religious concepts. A religious turn of mind is the preparation for sociability at a particular stage of life between death and rebirth. Here we also discover that those people who are unable to enter into religious feelings and connections are condemned to loneliness. We find people of like religious confessions grouped together.

"This is followed by a period when it is no longer sufficient to have lived within a religious community. A phase draws near when one can again feel loneliness. This period is a particularly important one between death and rebirth. Either we feel alone, even though we experienced togetherness with those of like religious confession, or we are able to bring understanding to every human soul in its essential character. For this communion we can only prepare by gaining an understanding of all religious confessions.

"Prior to the Mystery of Golgotha this was not necessary because the experiences in the spiritual world were different then. Christianity rightly understood bears within it the impulse to grasp all religious creeds and tendencies. One has gained an understanding of the Christ impulse only if one is able to grasp that the Christ is the only 'god' who descended to the Earth and gone through death.

"For one who has gained an understanding of the Christ down here on the Earth, the throne in the Sun will not be empty. This also enables him to recognize the nature of a particular encounter that occurs at this stage. The human being meets Lucifer, not as the 'tempter' but as a legitimate power who has to travel by his side if he is to progress in his journey. Qualities of the same nature in the wrong sphere have a destructive effect. The workings of Lucifer in the physical world are evil; but, after death, from the Sun sphere onwards, man needs Lucifer as a companion. He must meet Lucifer and Christ. Christ preserves his soul nature with the total assets that his soul has accumulated in previous incarnations. It is the task of the luciferic power to assist man so that he may also learn to apply the forces of the other hierarchical beings in the right manner for his next incarnation."

The Kamaloka Period of the After-Life

"Imagine the space between the Earth and the Moon, the spherical space described when the orbit of the Moon is taken as the outermost path away from the Earth. Then you have the realm in which man, loosened from the Earth, dwells during the Kamaloka period. When the Kamaloka period has been completed, a human being leaves this sphere and enters the actual celestial world. Things are reversed in relation to the physical plane. Here we are bound outwardly to the Earth, surrounded by the physical world and separated from the heavenly spheres. After death, the Earth is separated from us and we are united with the heavenly spheres. As long as we dwell within the Moon sphere, we are in Kamaloka, which means that we are still longing to be connected with the Earth. We proceed beyond it when we have learned through life in Kamaloka to forego passions and longings.

"In the first period of Kamaloka, the soul is clothed as in a cloud by its Imaginations. At first, the cloud is dark. When some time has elapsed after death, Imaginative vision gradually perceives that this cloud begins to light up as if irradiated by the rays of the morning Sun. When Inspiration is added to Imaginative cognition, we realize that we live, to begin with, in the cloud of our Earthly experiences. We are enveloped by them. We are able to relate ourselves only to those who have died and with whom we were together on the Earth, or to those still on Earth capable of ascending with their consciousness into the spiritual world. What we have characterized for Imaginative cognition as the illumination of the cloud of our visions from one side by a glimmering light, points to the approach of the hierarchies into our own being. We now begin to live into the realm of higher spirituality. Previously, we were only connected to the world we brought with us. Now the life of the higher hierarchies begins to shine towards us, to penetrate us.

"In later phases when Kamaloka has come to an end, we penetrate into still vaster realms. We expand ever more. When the Kamaloka phase draws to a close, man leaves behind him, as if removed, everything that during his physical existence was the expression of his propensities, longings, and desires for Earthly life. Man must experience all this but he must also relinquish it in the Moon sphere of Kamaloka. As man lives on after death, and later recalls the experiences in the Moon sphere, he will find all his Earthly emotions and passions inscribed there, that is, everything that developed in his soul life as a result of his positive attraction to the bodily nature. This is left behind in the Moon sphere and there it remains. It cannot be erased so easily. We carry it with us as an impulse, but it remains inscribed in the Moon sphere. The account of the debts, as it were, owing by every person is recorded in the Moon sphere."

The Venus Sphere

"After Kamaloka, we grow farther out into cosmic space into the whole planetary system, though first into what is called the Venus sphere. After the Kamaloka period, we become Venus dwellers. We are not now enclosed in such a small fraction of space as during our Earthly existence, but the wide sphere bound by the orbit of Venus is within our being.

"People who lack a moral disposition of soul on Earth become hermits in the Venus sphere. The morally inclined person, however, becomes what one might call a sociable being. There he will find above all the people with whom he had a close inner connection on Earth. This determines whether one is together with someone. It depends not on spatial relations, for we all fill the same space, but on our soul inclinations. We become hermits when we bring an unmoral disposition with us, and sociable beings, if we possess a moral inclination.

"In the Venus sphere a man has, above all, understanding for those with whom he was connected on Earth. If he had a moral attitude of soul, he will have real intercourse in the Venus sphere with those to whom he was related during his Earthly life.

"A person who has developed qualities of compassion and love—qualities that are usually termed moral—lives into the next sphere so that he becomes acquainted with the beings of that sphere. A man who brings a lack of morality into this realm dwells in it like a hermit. It may be best characterized by saying that morality prepared for us living socially together in the spiritual world. We are condemned to a fearful loneliness, filled with a continual longing to get to know others without being able to do so, as a result of a lack of morality in the physical world of the heart, as well as of the mind and will. Either as a hermit or as a sociable being who is a blessing in the spiritual world, do we dwell in this second sphere known as that of Venus.

"Now, man's being expands up to the orbits of Venus and Mercury, whereas previously it expanded only to the Moon. Something strange happens at this point. Until the Moon sphere, our involvement in Earthly matters is not entirely severed. We still know what we have done on the Earth, what we have thought. But recollection may be painful! On Earth, if we have done a person some injustice or have not loved him as much as we should, we can make up for these feelings. We can go to him and put things right. This is no longer possible from the Venus sphere onward. We behold the relationships in recollection. They remain but we cannot alter them.

"One lives in the Venus sphere in former relationships with people, and they cannot be altered. One looks back and unfolds what one has already developed. Through an immoral conception of life, we deprive ourselves of forces of attraction in the Venus sphere. Through an irreligious disposition of soul, we deprive ourselves of forces of attraction in the Mercury sphere. We cannot draw from this sphere the forces we need; which means that in the next incarnation we shall have an astral body that, in a certain respect, is imperfect.

"Thus, for a period after death man is still directly connected with the Earth. Then, he has to grow into and become a citizen of the spiritual world. This requires preparation. He first must possess a sensitivity and understanding for the spiritual world. Spiritual investigation observes a considerable difference after death between souls who have cultivated moral feelings and inclinations on Earth and those who have failed to do so. A person who has not developed moral feelings on Earth becomes a hermit after death. He will be unable to find his way both to other human beings and to the higher hierarchies.

"Consciousness is not extinguished then, and what awaits man is a sense of utter loneliness. From a certain period called the Venus period onward, man gains the possibility of living together with other beings by virtue of his moral life. We may say therefore that the way a person lives on Earth determines his existence in the Venus sphere, determines whether he experiences a dreadful hermit-like existence or establishes contact with other human souls or the beings of the higher hierarchies."

The Mercury Sphere

"At a later period, after having passed through the Venus sphere, we feel ourselves as Mercury dwellers. There between Venus and Mercury, where our 'cloud of visions' is irradiated from without, the Beings of the higher hierarchies are able to approach the human being. Now again it depends on whether we have prepared ourselves in the right manner to be received as social spirits into the ranks of the hierarchies and to have communion with them, or whether we are compelled to pass them by as hermits.

"Whether we are social or lonely spirits depends upon still another factor. Whereas in the previous sphere we can be sociable only if this has been prepared on Earth as a result of morality, in the Mercury sphere the power that leads us into community, into a kind of social life, is due to our religious attitude on Earth. We most certainly condemn ourselves to become hermits in the Mercury sphere if we have failed to develop religious feelings during earthly life, feelings of union with the Infinite, with the Divine.

Definite feelings for the spiritual that are colored by this or that religious creed bring it about that in the Mercury sphere a man has community only with those of like feelings who shared the same creed during Earthly life. In the Mercury sphere, individuals are separated according to their particular creeds.

"The ideas and conceptions are of a religious character. If religion has been a link between the transitory and the eternal, the life of soul in the Mercury sphere after death is different from what it is if there has been no such link. Again, whether we are sociable or isolated, hermit-like spirits depends upon whether we were or were not of a religious turn of mind during life on Earth. After death, an irreligious soul feels as though enclosed in a capsule, a prison. True, such a soul is aware that there are beings around him; but, he feels as though he were in a prison and unable to reach them.

"In the Mercury sphere we become hermits if on Earth we have had an irreligious disposition. We become sociable spirits if we bring a religious inclination with us. Inasmuch as in the physical world we are able to feel our devotion to the Holy Spirit, so in the Mercury sphere shall we find all those of a like inclination towards the divine spiritual. Men are grouped according to religious and philosophic trends in the Mercury sphere. On Earth it is so that both religious striving and religious experience still play a dominant part. In the Mercury sphere the grouping is purely according to religious confession and philosophic outlook. Those who share the same world-conception are together in large, powerful communities in the Mercury sphere. They are not hermits. Only those are hermits who have not been able to develop any religious feeling and experience. A person who has failed to develop religious feelings experiences himself as blind and dead in relation to everything that surrounds him.

"He who has something to bring becomes a social being, and he who has nothing to give is condemned to loneliness. A lack of religious inclination is dreadfully painful. The more religious the disposition of soul we have acquired, the more social we become in this sphere. People who lack religious inclination cut themselves off. They cannot move beyond a sheath or shell that surrounds them. Nevertheless, we get to know friends who are hermits; but, we cannot reach them. We continually feel as if we have to break through a shell; but, are incapable of doing so. In the Mercury sphere, if we have no religious inwardness, it is as if we were to freeze up."

The Sun and the Mystery of Golgotha in the After-Life

"After the Mercury sphere, this is followed by a sphere which expands up to the Sun. We are connected with the Sun. There is a period between death and rebirth when we become Sun beings. But now something further is necessary. In the first sphere, Venus, we need moral inclination and in the Mercury sphere, a religious life. In the Sun sphere it is essential that we truly know the nature and being of the Sun spirits and above all, the ruling Sun Spirit, the Christ, and that we made a connection with Him on Earth.

"Since the Mystery of Golgotha, humanity has naïvely endeavored to draw towards the Christ. In our time, spiritual science must bring an understanding of the Sun Being to the world. Through the understanding given by means of spiritual science, what was brought by the lofty Sun Spirit, by the Christ, the Christ Who came down and through the Mystery of Golgotha has become the Spirit of the Earth will be retrieved.

"If we understand the Mystery of Golgotha and realize what happened there, then in the Sun sphere we become sociable spirits. As soon as we have gone beyond the Moon sphere, we are spiritually surrounded by visions. Now the spiritual beings of the higher hierarchies illumine us. It is as if the Sun rose and irradiated the clouds in the Sun sphere. Just as we only learn to know the spiritual hierarchies in the Mercury sphere if we have a religious inclination, so in the Sun sphere we must be permeated by a Christian mood of soul.

"In the Venus sphere we are, more or less, limited to the circle of those with whom we were related on Earth. In the Mercury sphere we feel at home with those who had similar religious experiences to ours on Earth and we still find satisfaction only among these communities. But the soul is conscious of deep loneliness in the Sun sphere if it has no understanding for the souls entering this sphere.

"In ancient times, conditions were such that in the Mercury sphere souls were to be found in the provinces of the several religions, finding and giving understanding in them. Because all religions have sprung from a common source, when the human being entered the Sun sphere he had in him so much of the old common inheritance that he could come near to all the other souls in the Sun sphere and be together with them, to understand them, to be a social spirit among them. The Christ impulse affords the possibility of understanding every human experience. Christianity is a general religion, valid for all people.

"In the Sun period, we have gradually entered a realm in which we are dependent on spiritual light. Previously, before the

Sun period, we still experienced the after-effects of the Earth, the after-effects of what we have been personally, including our moral and religious feelings. Now we require more than these. Now we require the faculty to see what is in the spiritual world; but, this cannot be prepared for on Earth. We have to journey through realms of forces of which we cannot know anything here on Earth.

"The Mystery of Golgotha signifies the re-enlivening of man's consciousness precisely during the middle period between death and rebirth. If we have experienced on Earth an understanding of Christ and the Mystery of Golgotha and have established a relationship to them, this will implant into us thoughts and forces that maintain our consciousness during this period after death.

"Naturally, every man returns through a new birth to Earth; but it is of importance whether the consciousness has been extinguished or whether it has remained intact across the abyss. If we reach the Sun sphere after death with a knowledge of the Mystery of Golgotha, we are able to look backward and remember that with all that is essentially human in us, we have come from God. We also experience that we have been able to save our consciousness because of our understanding of the Mystery of Golgotha, and that we can develop our consciousness further as we behold this Spirit now drawing near to us.

"On reaching the stage where the recollections of the Mystery of Golgotha is needed in order to maintain consciousness, however, a great transformation begins. We are then no longer able to hold the previous visions. For example, until this phase we can speak in terms of astral color phenomena in this realm and of the visionary images of beings surrounding us. Midway between death and a new birth visions and recollections fall away, we lose our connection with them, and they separate themselves off from our being. Only what bridges the differences between the various religious confessions can help us in the Sun sphere. What is needed is an understanding that enables us not only to come together with those of a like confession, but also to form a relationship with humanity as a whole.

"In the Sun sphere, a thorough understanding of the Christ impulse is essential. We must bring this understanding along with us from the Earth; for Christ once did dwell in the Sun but, as we know, He descended from the Sun and united Himself with the Earth. We have to carry Him up to the Sun period, and then we can become sociable beings through the Christ impulse and learn to understand Him in the sphere of the Sun."

Christ and Lucifer in the After-Life

"The understanding of Christ that we bring with us from the Earth leads us as far as the Sun sphere. There it acts as a guide, so to speak, irrespective of creed or confession. But we encounter another being in the Sun sphere who utters words that have virtually the same content. That being is Lucifer. We must have acquired on Earth an understanding of the difference between Christ and Lucifer; for Lucifer is now to accompany us through the further spheres between death and rebirth.

"At this stage, one feels oneself drawing away from the Earth. The Earth is far away below one, and journeying into the spirit world one feels that one has reached the Sun. Just as during earthly life we feel ourselves linked to the Earth, so now we feel at one with the Sun with its whole planetary system.

"We must now confront, and need to understand, the being known as Lucifer. The sensation in the Sun is not one of being surrounded by streaming physical light, but of dwelling in the pure light of the spirit. From this moment onward, one experiences Lucifer no longer as an antagonistic being. On the contrary, he appears more and more to be fully justified in the world. One now senses the urge, in the further course of the life after death, to recognize Christ and Lucifer side by side as equally justifiable powers. However strange the equal importance of Christ and Lucifer may appear, this insight is reached from this stage onward, and one comes to see these two powers more or less as brothers.

"Our interest in people with whom we have been connected wanes, and we lose interest in things. We realize that the recollections we still have at this point are carried forward only by the Christ. Christ accompanies us, and as a result we are capable of remembering. If Christ were not to accompany us, our recollection of earthly life would vanish because it is the experience of uniting ourselves with Christ that beyond this point connects us with the Earth.

"Through a further stage in the spiritual world, we gain a totally new interest in Lucifer and his realm. Severed from earthly interests, we can now experience the confrontation of Lucifer absolutely without danger. We make the remarkable discovery that Lucifer's influence is harmful to us only when we are entangled in earthly affairs. He now appears as the being who illumines what we have to undergo later in the world of the spirit. For a long span of time, we feel that we must acquire what Lucifer can bestow upon us in these realms of the spirit world.

"As Christ-filled beings, we live into the Sun sphere. As we proceed further, we enter into a realm where the Sun is now below us, as previously was the Earth. We look back towards the Sun, and this is the beginning of something strange. We become aware that we have to recognize yet another being, the spirit of Lucifer.

"It is only when we arrive beyond the Sun sphere that we recognize him as he was before he became Lucifer, when he was still a brother of Christ. Lucifer changed only in the course of time because he remained behind and severed himself from the stream of cosmic progress. His harmful influence does not extend beyond the Sun sphere. Above this there is still another sphere where Lucifer can unfold his activity as it was before the severance. He does not unfold anything harmful there, and if we have united ourselves rightly with the Mystery of Golgotha, we journey onward led by Christ and are rightly received by Lucifer into yet further spheres of the universe. The Sun is below us and so is the light of the Sun. Now we need a new light-bearer who illumines our path into the Universe.

"So you see, we go through the Moon, Mercury, Venus, and Sun spheres and in each sphere we meet, to begin with, what corresponds to the inner forces that we bring with us. Our emotions, urges, passions, sensual love, unite us to the Moon sphere. In the Venus sphere we meet everything that is due to our moral imperfections; in the Mercury sphere all our religious shortcomings; in the Sun sphere, everything that severs us from the purely human.

"Now we proceed to the spheres of Mars, Jupiter, and Saturn. Here Lucifer is our guide, and we enter into a realm that bestows new forces upon us. Now, we have the Sun below us. We grow into the divine-spiritual world, and as we do so we must hold fast in memory what we have brought with us of the Christ impulse. We can only acquire this on Earth and the more deeply we have done so, the farther we can carry it into the Cosmos. Now Lucifer draws near to us. He leads us out into a realm we must cross in order to be prepared for a new incarnation. There is one thing we cannot dispense with unless Lucifer is to become a threat to us, and that is the understanding of the Christ impulse, of what we have heard about Christ during our life on Earth. Lucifer approaches us out of his own accord during the period between birth and death; but Christ must be received during Earthly life.

"We then grow into the other spheres beyond the Sun. We become ever larger, so to speak. Below us we have the Sun and above, the mighty, vast expanse of the Starry heavens. We grow into the great cosmic realm up to a certain boundary, and as we grow outward cosmic forces work upon us from all directions. We receive forces from the mighty world of the stars into our widespread being.

"We would wander in darkness if Lucifer were not to approach us. However, we can only walk beside him if we are guided by the Christ. Together they lead man after the Sun period in subsequent forms of life, that is, through the Mars, Jupiter and Saturn periods. During the times following the Sun period, man is brought together with forces that he requires for his next incarnation.

"It is in the Sun sphere between death and the new birth that again and again we hear the words spoken to our soul with all their force: *Thou art a God, be as a God!* We know with all certainty when we arrive in the Sun sphere that Lucifer meets us again and impresses the meaning of this utterance forcibly upon us. From then onwards we can understand Lucifer very well; but Christ only if on Earth we have prepared ourselves to understand Him. Christ's utterance will have no meaning for us in the Sun sphere if by our relationship on Earth to the mystery of Golgotha we have not gained some understanding of it.

"Trivial as the following words may be, let me say this: In the Sun sphere we find two thrones. From the throne of Lucifer—which is always occupied—there sound the words of temptation, asserting our divinity. The second throne seems to us—or rather to many human beings—to be still empty; for on this other throne in the Sun sphere between death and the new birth, we have to discover what can be called the Akashic picture of Christ. If we can find the Akashic picture of Christ it will be for us a blessing. But it has become possible to find that picture only because Christ came down from the Sun and has united Himself with the Earth and because we have been able to open our eyes of spirit here on Earth through understanding in some measure the Mystery of Golgotha. This will ensure that the throne of Christ in the Sun sphere does not appear empty to us; but that the deeds He performed while His dwelling-place was still the Sun sphere become visible. As I said, I have to use trivial words in speaking of these two thrones; this sublime fact can only be spoken of figuratively. But anyone who acquires more and more understanding will realize that words coined on Earth are inadequate and that one is obliged to resort to imagery in order to be intelligible."

The Mars Sphere

"After we have felt ourselves to be Sun dwellers, having left the Earth behind us, we now leave the Sun sphere and experience ourselves in our cosmic reality as inhabitants of Mars. In fact, for this phase it appears as if Christ had given us everything relating to the past and that Lucifer prepares us for our future incarnation. If this Mars sphere is experienced consciously, we discover that Lucifer bestows on us all experiences not originating in the earthly sphere that we carry within us through the width of the Cosmos. Lucifer gives us everything unrelated to the Earth. Our former human interest becomes more and more cosmic. Whereas previously we absorbed on Earth what the mineral, the plant, the animal, air and water, mountain and valley gave us, we gather from this point onward the experiences that reach us from the Cosmos. It is a form of perception that has always been known, but little understood, as the 'harmony of the spheres.' We perceive everything as harmonies rather than the separate sounds of the physical world.

"Without exception, all materialistically inclined people become hermits once they have gone beyond the Sun into the Mars sphere.

"Spiritually, man lives in the Mars sphere as indicated. Then he proceeds further and lives into the Jupiter sphere. His connection with the Earth, which up until now still continued slightly, has become quite meaningless. The Sun still has a limited influence on him, but now the Cosmos begins to work powerfully upon him. Everything is now working from outside, and man receives cosmic influences. The entire Cosmos works through the harmony of the spheres, which assumes even other forms the further we investigate life between death and rebirth. It is not easy to characterize the change that occurs in the harmony of the spheres as it cannot be expressed in words."

The Jupiter Sphere

"We now leave the realm of Mars, and the seer denotes the next sphere as Jupiter. At a certain point we experience ourselves at the center of the Universe. From all sides we perceive the cosmic facts through the harmony of the spheres. As we proceed, the harmony of the spheres increases in volume. Finally, it is so powerful that we are numbed by it. Stupefied, we lift into the harmony of the spheres.

"The harmony of the spheres transforms itself in the passage from Mars to Jupiter as orchestral music would change into choral music. Jupiter transforms into choral music. It becomes increasingly tone, filled with meaning, expressive of its actual being. The harmony of the spheres receives content as we ascend into the sphere of Jupiter, and in the Saturn sphere full content is bestowed upon it as the expression of the Cosmic Word out of which everything has been created and which is found in the *Gospel of St. John*, 'In the beginning was the Word.' In this Word, cosmic order and cosmic wisdom sound forth."

The Saturn Sphere

"After we have gone through the Jupiter sphere our existence reaches Saturn, the outermost limit of the solar system. At this juncture we undergo an important experience of a moral nature. If Christ has preserved our memory of earlier conditions on Earth and protected us from the states of fear arising out of a waning consciousness, we realize, particularly in our present soul configuration, how little our life on Earth was attuned to higher moral demands, to the majesty of the entire cosmic existence. Our past earthly life rises up reproachfully out of an undifferentiated darkness, the sum total of the last incarnation as it formed itself karmically during that life appears before the soul.

"In fact, the overall picture of your present incarnation corresponds to what now arises in your soul at this state after death; but, everything you have to object to in your own last incarnation is poignantly experienced. We behold our last earthy life from a cosmic viewpoint.

"From this time onward, neither the Christ principle nor Lucifer can maintain our consciousness. Unless an initiation took place in a previous Earth life, consciousness is definitely dimmed. It marks a necessary spiritual sleep-like condition following the consciousness that prevailed until then. This spiritual sleep is connected with another factor. Because all feelings and the capacity to form ideas have ceased, the total cosmic forces, with the exception of those emanating from the solar system, can now act directly upon the person. Imagine the whole of the solar system out of action and only the forces outside it working. This will give you a picture of the influences that now begin to be operative."

The Return to Another Birth

Once a person has gone through the life review in backward order and has expanded outwardly through the seven spheres reviewing their karmic "book of life", there comes the moment called the Sun at Midnight. The individual then has a chance to, so to speak, stand upon the rings of Saturn and look out at the celestial sphere of the stars and truly perceive their original spiritual home. The aspirant has now returned to the throne of God and witnesses the host of spiritual hierarchies singing in unison the cosmic heartbeat of the Universe. The Harmony of the Spheres is below the aspirant and the Heavenly Celestial Sphere is above them.

The aspirant stands in a majestic pause in time before turning around and beginning the process of contraction back through the seven spheres, back to the Earth and a new human body created by the gifts they gather from each sphere as they contract into their next incarnation, their next physical birth. It is in that celestial moment of pause, that rest period, between expanding and contracting that one can truly understand the polarity of incarnation and excarnation, life and death, inwardness and outwardness. The point of singularity between inner and outer, your "I Am", can now perceive the cycle of repeated human incarnations and the myriad effects of the wheel of karma. After witnessing these spiritually cosmic processes of life and death, the aspirant begins to appreciate the wisdom found in the slow and gradual process of the human being growing into what Rudolf Steiner described as a "Spirit of Freedom and Love" through graduation from the Earth Planetary Condition in preparation for becoming an Angel in the Future Jupiter Planetary Condition.

> "For in the resurrection they neither marry, nor are given in marriage, but are as the angels of God in heaven."
> *Matthew* (22:30)

As the Sun at Midnight is experienced, the 'eternal song' of the *Book of Revelation* is sounding from all directions of space to the spirit of the individual and, for a moment, the individual and the Cosmos are One. In that moment of longing for the divine, the individual spirit understands the long path from a child-like human being to a celestial, cosmic Angel, like the spirits who now create the symphony of the Harmonies of the Spheres and the ever-present pulse-beat of the Cosmos enveloping them in the undulating cosmic ether of Akasha.

I can imagine that it is sometimes hard for an initiate, who is still consciously awake at the turning point of excarnation, the 'ring pass not' of Saturn, to turn around and go back down the path they have just finished coming up. To turn around from the celestial and return to the terrestrial must be great pain for those who know the Language of the Spirit and yet return to the cold, dark, 'muddy vesture of decay.' What yearning for the spirit must fill their hearts? But ultimately, the love of humanity stirs in them the vow of the bodhisattva, the vow of Quan Yin, to reach the gates of heaven but not go through those gates until all other sentient beings are helped to enter first. Thus, the initiate returns to Earth to give a helping hand to those just climbing up to the first rung of the ladder to Heaven.

Life Between Death and Rebirth, by Rudolf Steiner

"Beyond Saturn, a spiritual sleep begins whereas during the previous stages one was spiritually awake. From now onward consciousness is dimmed, the human being dwells in a benumbed condition that makes it possible for him to undergo still other experiences. Just as in sleep we do away with tiredness and gather new forces, so as a result of the dimming of consciousness, when we have become a fully expanded spatial sphere, spiritual forces stream in from the Cosmos.

"First, we have sensed it, then we have heard it as a universal orchestra. Then it has Sung forth and we have perceived it as the Word. Then we fall asleep, and it penetrates us. During this period, we again travel through all the spheres; but, with a dimmed consciousness. Our consciousness becomes ever dimmer. We now contract, quickly or slowly according to our karma, and during this process of contraction we come once more under the influence of the forces emanating from the Sun system. We journey back from sphere to sphere through the Cosmos. Now we are not sensitive to influences from the Moon sphere. We proceed, unaffected, unhampered, as it were, and continue to contract until we unite ourselves with the small human germ that goes through its development before birth.

"Unless physiology and embryology receive their facts from spiritual scientific investigation, they cannot contain the truth; for the embryo is a reflection of the vast Cosmos. The whole Cosmos is carried within it. The human being carries as a potential power within him what happens physically between conception and birth, and also what he undergoes during the period of cosmic sleep.

"Life between death and rebirth falls into two parts. To begin with it is unalterable. We ascend, the beings approach us. We enter into a condition of sleep and then change can occur. The forces now enter with which we are born. Considering the evolution of man in this way, we see that the human being after death first lives in a world of visions. He only learns to recognize later what he really is as a soul-spiritual being. Beings approach us from outside and they illumine us as the golden light of the morning illuminates the things of the outer world. Thus, we ascend, and the spiritual world penetrates into us. We do not live in the spiritual world from outside until we have become mature enough to experience what we are in our visionary world, until we encounter the beings of the spiritual world who approach us from all sides like rays.

"It is when the human being ascends into the spiritual world that the light of spiritual beings draws near to him. But there is one moment when he is clearly visible, illumined by the light of the hierarchies so that he reflects back the whole of the outer world. The entire Cosmos now appears as if reflected by man. You can imagine the process. First you live on as a cloud that is not sufficiently illumined, then you ray back the light of the Cosmos and then you dissolve. There is a moment when man reflects back the cosmic light. Up to this point he can ascend.

"We reach a boundary, then we begin to contract and enter again into the realms through which we have traveled previously. We go through the Sun, Mercury, Venus, and Moon spheres until we come again into the neighborhood of the Earth and everything that has been carried out in the cosmic expanse has concentrated itself again in an embryo borne by an Earthly mother.

"This is the mystery of man's nature between death and a new birth. After he has gone through the gate of death he expands ever more from the small space of the Earth to the realms of Moon, Venus, Mercury, Sun, Mars, Jupiter, and Saturn. We have then grown into cosmic space, like giant spheres. After we, as souls, have received the forces of the universe, of the stars, we contract again and carry the forces of the starry world within us. This explains how in the concentrated brain structure an imprint of the total starry heavens may be found.

"Why do I use the terms Mercury, Venus, Sun, Mars, Jupiter, and Saturn for the periods after death? When man has gone through the gate of death he expands more and more. In fact, life after death is such that one knows oneself to be spread out over a vast space. This expansion goes so far that one finally occupies the space bound by the orbit of the Moon. Then one grows out to the orbit of Mercury in the occult sense, then out to the orbits of Venus, Sun, and Mars. One grows out into the vast celestial spaces. But the spatial togetherness of the many human souls is not significant. When you permeate the whole of the Venus sphere this is also the case for the others, but it does not mean that because of this you are aware of them. Even if one knows that one is not alone, one can still feel lonely.

"Finally, one expands into the universe in a sphere circumscribed by the orbit of Saturn and beyond. As one grows in this way one gathers the forces needed to build up the next incarnation. Then one returns. One becomes ever smaller until one unites oneself again with the Earth.

"Between death and rebirth, man expands into the whole Cosmos and however strange it may appear, when we return to the Earth we bring all the forces of the solar system with us into life and unite them with what is inherited out of the physical substances. By means of cosmic forces we build up our physical body and our brain. Here, between birth and death we dwell within the narrow confines of our physical body. After death, we live expanded into the entire solar macrocosm.

"The one person has a deep moral sense, the other less so. The one who on Earth had a deep moral sense goes through the spiritual world in such a way that he can experience everything as a sociable being. The power for this flows from the starry realms. Another who is not thus prepared is unable to make any connections and because he did not bring any spiritualized forces with him, he also is unable to receive any moral predispositions. He will journey alone through the various spheres."

Preparing for the Next Incarnation

"Let us now consider the important relationship between the second phase of life after death and the embryonic period. You know that embryonic life begins with a small spherical germ. We can make the remarkable observation that in its earliest stages the embryo represents a mirror-picture of all the human being experiences out of the Cosmos. At the outset, the human germ carries a mirror-picture of cosmic existence from which its life in the solar system is excluded. It is remarkable that during the further stages of embryonic development all cosmic influences are rejected except those emanating from the solar system. These are absorbed by the embryo. Hereditary forces commence their activity on the embryo at a comparatively later stage when, during life after death, we have retraced our steps via Saturn, Jupiter, and Mars. Therefore, it may be said that the germ is already prepared by man during cosmic existence in a condition of universal sleep and before the embryonic period.

"Then, the later embryonic conditions find their mirror-image in the early phase of prenatal life, and the early conditions of embryonic existence find their reflection in a later phase before conception. So, we obtain a spiritual mirror-picture in reverse of embryonic development. Here is the embryo in the one direction, and for each phase in the one direction I find a mirror-image in the other. The two sides are related as object and mirror-image, and conception marks the point at which the mirror-images arise.

"Life between death and a new birth is full of content, but one thing is missing. We do in fact recapitulate everything we have experienced from the previous incarnation until the present one. We sense cosmic being, but during the first stage of life after death we do not experience what has happened on the Earth between the two incarnations. Until we reach the Sun sphere, we are so preoccupied with our memories of life before death that our interest in events on the Earth is completely diverted.

"We live with those individuals who also are dwelling in the spiritual world after death. We are fully involved in the relationships that we have with them on Earth and shape these connections to fit their ultimate consequences. During this period our interest is continually diverted and thereby lessened for those who are still on the Earth. Only when those who remain on Earth seek us with their souls can a link with them be created. This should be considered an important moral element that throws light upon the connection between the living and the dead.

"A person who has died before us and whom we completely forget, finds it difficult to reach us here in earthly life. The love, the constant sympathy we feel for the dead, creates a path on which a connection with earthly life is established. During the early stages after death, those who have passed on can live with us only out of this connection. Those who have passed on can reach us most easily if they can find thoughts and feelings directed toward them from the Earth.

"The situation is different for the second stage between death and a new birth. We are then so deeply involved in cosmic interests that it becomes exceedingly difficult to establish a connection with the Earth during this second period. Apart from the interest we take in the Cosmos, we wish to cooperate in the right shaping of our further karma. In addition to our cosmic impressions, we retain best what we have to correct karmically, and we help to shape a next life that will help to compensate for the karmic debts incurred.

"During this period, we want to return to life with all our strength in order to correct our karma. We forget all too easily after the cosmic sleep described, when we awaken into the present, that we actually want to reincarnate. Just as we are strengthened through sleep in earthly life and endowed with new forces, so as a result of the described cosmic sleep are we equipped with forces for our new incarnation.

"During spirit-existence between death a new birth, we are in fact old to begin with, and we become children in relation to the spiritual life during the second period. Spiritual life flows in the reverse order. To begin with, we carry the errors and shortcomings of earthly life into the spiritual world. Then gradually, during the cosmic existence, they are removed.

"Ultimately, you will refer the being of God to yourself, to let it be reflected in you. Such a stage arises after death when gazing back on man. The surroundings are reflected in him, even the Godhead. Life after death is the reflection of the divine. It is well known that Dante said that during one's existence in the spiritual world a point comes where one 'beholds the divine as man.'

"What could be more uplifting than to know that we can discover the fount of our life between death and rebirth. We can discover our kinship with the whole Universe! What could give us greater strength for our duties in life than the knowledge that we bear within us the forces pouring in from the universe and must so prepare ourselves in life that these forces can become active in us when, between death and rebirth, we pass into the spheres of the planets and of the Sun."

Building a New Body

"Man builds his entire body both from the movements of the stars and from the constellations of the stars in the great Universe. The human body is indeed an image of the world of stars. Much of the work we have to do between death and new birth consists in the building of our own body from the Universe. The human being as he stands on Earth is indeed a shrunken Universe.

"Moreover, his life of soul and spirit between death and re-birth consists in working with the spiritual Beings—working at the super-sensible form of man, which is created first in the etheric and astral realms and only then shrinks and contracts till it is able to be clothed in physical material.

"Only if we can understand how the soul-and-spirit, having thus lost itself in language, becomes one with the world of stars and then recovers itself from the world of stars,—only then do we apprehend the complete cycle of human life between death and a new birth.

"For if we have the faculty to concentrate in a single point within the heart and thence to turn ourselves inside out in spirit, we simply do become the Universe which in the normal course we experience between death and a new birth. Such is the secret of the inner man. It is only in the physical world that he cannot be turned inside out. The heart of man however is in effect a Universe turned inside out, and that is how the physical and Earthly world is really joined to the spiritual."

Theosophical Terms Concerning the After-life

The following selection by Rudolf Steiner is the last of ten lectures in the lecture series *Between Death and Rebirth* (GA 141) which clarifies his usage of Theosophical terms found in his book *Theosophy*. The terms for each of the spheres that the soul traverses in the after-life, are here aligned with the selections presented above from *Life Between Death and Rebirth*. For those interested in comparing the two versions, this is the best lecture that clarifies Theosophical and Anthroposophical terminology in relationship to the planetary spheres that are experienced in sleep and death. Steiner is keen to point out that both schemes agree perfectly. Some may find the older Theosophical terms difficult to understand; but, it is well worth the study. These selections are not as appropriate to read to the dead as are the selections from *Life Between Birth and Death* found above.

    The selections below are a beautiful example of the development of Steiner's thought that coincided with Eastern terminology and yet was transformed and delivered in a Western esoteric format. The presentation below is not as picturesque or poetic as the selections from *Life Between Birth and Death* and yet they present a concise, clear, and comprehensive Imagination of these planetary realms. They are offered to give a well-rounded understanding of Dr. Steiner's indications concerning the life after death.

Selections from *Theosophy,* by Rudolf Steiner

"In the book *Theosophy*, there is a description of the passage of the soul after death through the Soul-World. This Soul-World is divided into a region of 'Burning Desires' a region of 'Flowing Susceptibility', a region of 'Wishes', a region of 'Attraction and Repulsion' (Lust und Unlust), and then into the higher regions of 'Soul-Light', of 'Active Soul-Force', and the true 'Soul-Life.' That was how the Soul-World through which the soul has to pass after death was described. Thereafter, the soul has to pass through what is described as the Spirit-Land and this sphere, too, with its successive regions, is described in the book *Theosophy* by using certain earthly images: the 'continental' region of Spirit-land, the 'oceanic' region, and so forth.

"In the course of these lectures, descriptions have been given of how the soul, having passed through the gate of death, lays aside the physical body, then the etheric body, and then expands and expands, lives through regions which for reasons that were explained may be called the region of the Moon, then that of Venus, of Mercury, of the Sun, of Mars, of Jupiter, of Saturn, and then of the starry firmament itself. The soul or, let us say, the actual spiritual individuality of the human being concerned, continually expands, lives through these regions which enclose ever more extensive cosmic spaces and then begins to contract, becoming smaller and smaller, in order finally to unite with the seed which comes to it from the stream of heredity.

"And through this union of the human seed which the individual acquired through heredity with what has been absorbed from the great macrocosmic spheres, there arises the human being who is to embark on the course of earthly life, the being who is to live through his existence between birth and death.

"Now as a matter of fact, what was said in the book *Theosophy* and in the lectures was fundamentally the same, and your attention has been called to this. In *Theosophy* the description was given in certain pictures more closely related to inner conditions of the soul. In the lectures given here during the Winter, the descriptions dealt with the great cosmic relationships connected with the functions of the several planets. It is now a matter of harmonizing the two descriptions.

"During the first period after death the soul has to look back upon what was experienced on Earth. The period of Kamaloka, or call it what you will, is a period during which the soul's life is still concerned entirely with earthly conditions. Kamaloka is fundamentally a period during which the soul feels bound to disengage itself gradually from any direct connections still persisting from the last incarnation on Earth. In the physical body on Earth, the soul has experiences which depend upon the bodily life, indeed very largely upon sense-impressions. If you 'think away' everything that sense-impressions bring into the soul and then try to realize how much still remains in it, you will have a picture of a very meagre content indeed! And yet on final consideration you will be able to say: When the soul passes through the gate of death, everything given by the senses comes to an end and whatever is left can at most only be memories of earlier sense-impressions. If, therefore, you think about how much of what is yielded by sense-impressions is left in the soul, it will be easy for you to form an idea of what remains of these impressions after death.

"Recall any sense-impressions experienced, for example, yesterday, while they are still comparatively vivid, and you will realize how pale they have already become compared with their former vividness; that will give you some idea of how little of what the sense-impressions have conveyed is left to the soul as remembrance. This shows you that basically all the soul's life in the world of the senses is specifically earthly experience. When the sense-organs fall away at death, all significance of the sense-impressions falls away as well. But because the human being still clings to his sense-impressions and retains a longing for them, the first region through which he passes in the life after death is the region of Burning Desires. He would like still to have sense-impressions for a long time after death; but, this is impossible because he has discarded the sense-organs. The life spent longing for sense-impressions and being unable to enjoy them is life in the region of Burning Desires. It is a life that does actually burn within the soul and is part of the existence in Kamaloka; the soul longs for sense-impressions to which it was accustomed on Earth and—because the sense-organs have been laid aside—cannot have them.

"A second region of life in Kamaloka is that of Flowing Susceptibility. When the soul lives through this region it has already ceased to long for sense-impressions but still longs for thoughts, for thoughts which in life on Earth are acquired through the instrumentality of the brain. In the region of Burning Desires the soul gradually realizes that it is nonsense to wish for sense-impressions in a world for the experience of which the necessary sense-organs have been discarded, a world in which no being can possibly have sense-organs formed entirely of substance of the Earth. The soul may long since have ceased to yearn for sense-impressions but still longs to think in the way that is customary on Earth. This Earthly thinking is discarded in the region of Flowing Susceptibility. There, the human being gradually recognizes that thoughts such as are formed on Earth have significance only in the life between birth and death.

"At this stage, when the human being has weaned himself from fostering thoughts that are dependent upon the physical instrument of the brain, he is still aware of a certain connection with the Earth through what is contained in his Wishes. After all, wishes are connected with the soul more intimately than thoughts. Wishes have their own distinctive coloring in every individual. Whereas thoughts differ in youth, in middle life and in old age, a particular form of wishing continues throughout a man's Earthly life. This form and coloring of wishes are only later discarded in the region of Wishes.

"And then finally, in the region of Attraction and Repulsion, man rids himself of all longing to be connected with a physical body, with the physical body which was his in the last incarnation. While a man is passing through these regions, of Burning Desires, of Flowing Susceptibility, of Wishes, of Attraction and Repulsion, a certain longing for the last Earthly life is still present.

"First, in the region of Burning Desires the soul still longs to be able to see through eyes, to hear through ears, although eyes and ears no longer exist. When the soul has finally cast off any such longing, it still yearns to be able to think by means of a brain such as was available on Earth. Having got rid of this longing too, there still remains the desire to wish with a heart as on Earth. Finally, the human being ceases to long for sense-impressions or for thoughts formed by his brain or for wishes of his heart; but, a hankering for his last incarnation on Earth taken as a whole, still lingers. Gradually, however, he then rids himself of this longing too.

"You will find that all the experiences in these regions correspond exactly with the passage of the expanding soul into the region called the Mercury sphere, an expansion through the

Moon sphere into the Venus sphere. On approaching the Venus sphere, however, the soul encounters conditions described in the book *Theosophy* as a kind of spiritual region of the Soul-World.

"Read the description of the passage of the soul through this region and you will see from what is said about the kind of experiences undergone there that what is generally called the unpleasant element of Kamaloka already comes to an end in the region of Soul-Light. This region of Soul-Light corresponds with what I have said about the Venus sphere. If you compare what was said about the life of the soul when it has expanded to the Venus sphere with what is contained in the book *Theosophy* about the region of Soul-Light, you will realize that endeavors were made to describe this region first from the aspect of inner influences of the soul and then from the aspect of the great macrocosmic conditions through which the soul passes.

"If you read what is said in *Theosophy* about the 'Active Soul-Force', you will realize that the inner experiences undergone in that region are in keeping with what is decisive during the passage through the Mercury sphere. It has been said that if the soul is to pass in the right way through the Mercury sphere it must have developed certain religious impulses during earthly life. In order to progress through the Mercury sphere with companionship and not in compulsory isolation, the soul must be imbued with certain religious concepts. Compare what was said about this with the description given in the book *Theosophy* of the region of Active Soul-Force and you will find that they agree, that in one case the inner aspect of the conditions was described, in the other, the outer aspect.

"The highest region of the Soul-World, the region of pure Soul-Life, is experienced by the soul in passing through the region of the Sun. So, we can say that the sphere of existence in

Kamaloka extends to and somewhat beyond the Moon sphere; then the more luminous regions of the Soul-World begin and extend to the sphere of the Sun. The soul experiences in the Sun sphere the region of true Soul-Life. We know that in the Sun sphere after death the soul comes into contact with the Light-Spirit, with Lucifer, who on Earth has become the tempter, the corrupter.

"When the soul has expanded into the Cosmos it comes more and more closely into contact with those forces which now enable it to develop what is needed for the next incarnation on Earth. Not until the soul has passed through the region of the Sun has it finished with the last earthly incarnation. As far as the region of Attraction and Repulsion is concerned, that is to say the region between the Moon and Venus, the soul is still burdened inwardly with yearning for the last life on Earth; moreover, even in the regions of Venus, Mercury, and the Sun the soul is not yet completely free from the ties of the last incarnation. But then it must finally have finished even with everything that transcends merely personal experience; in the Venus region with whatever moral concepts have or have not been acquired, in the region of Mercury with whatever religious conceptions have been developed, in the region of the Sun with whatever understanding has been acquired of the 'human-universal' quality in existence—that which is not confined to any particular religious creed but is concerned with a religious life befitting all mankind. Thus, it is even the higher interests that can develop in the further evolution of humanity with which the soul has finished by the time it enters into the region of the Sun.

"Then the soul passes into cosmic-spiritual life and finds its place in the Mars region. This region corresponds with what is described in *Theosophy* as the first sphere of the 'Spirit-Land.' This description portrays the inner aspect of the fact that the soul is spiritual to the extent of being able to behold as something external to itself the 'archetype', as it were, of the physical bodily organization and of physical conditions on the Earth in general. The archetypes of physical life on Earth appear as a kind of 'continental' mass of the Spirit-Land. The external configurations of a man's different incarnations are inscribed in this 'continental' region. There we have a picture of what, in terms of cosmic existence, the human soul has to experience in the Mars region.

"It might seem strange that this Mars region, which has repeatedly been described in these lectures as a region of strife, should be said to be the first region of Devachan, of the true Spirit-Land. Nevertheless, this is the case. Everything that on Earth belongs to the actual material realm and causes the mineral kingdom to appear as a purely material realm is due to the fact that on Earth the forces are engaged in perpetual conflict among themselves. This also led to the result that at the time when materialism was in its prime and material life was assumed to be the sole reality, the 'struggle for existence' was regarded as the only valid law of life on Earth. That is, of course, an error, because material existence is not the only form of existence evolving on Earth. But when the human being assumes embodiment on Earth, he can only enter into the form of existence that has its archetypes in the lowest region of what is, for the Earth, the Spirit-Land.

"Read the description of the lowest region of Spirit-Land as given in the book *Theosophy*. I want to quote this particular chapter today in connection with our present studies. Towards the beginning of the description of the Spirit-Land you will find the following passage:

"The development of the spirit in Spirit-Land takes place through the man throwing himself completely into the life of the different regions of this land.

"His own life as it were dissolves into each region successively; he takes on, for the time being, their characteristics. Through this they permeate his being with theirs, in order that his being may be able to work, strengthened by theirs, in his earthly life. In the first region of the Spirit-Land, man is surrounded by the spiritual archetypes of earthly things. During life on Earth, he learns to know only the shadows of these archetypes which he grasps in his thoughts. What is merely thought on the Earth is in this region experienced, lived. Man moves among thoughts; but these thoughts are real beings.

"Our own embodiments dissolve here into a unity with the rest of the world. Thus, here we look upon the archetypes of the physical, corporeal reality as a unity, to which we have ourselves belonged. We learn, therefore, gradually to know our relationship, our unity, with the surrounding world, by observation. We learn to say to it: 'That which is here spread out around thee, thou art that.' And that is one of the fundamental thoughts of ancient Indian Vedanta wisdom. The sage acquires, even during his earthly life, what others experience after death, namely, ability to grasp the thought that he himself is related to all things, the thought, 'Thou art that.' In earthly life this is an ideal to which the thought-life can be devoted; in the Land of Spirit it is an immediate reality, one which grows ever clearer to us through spiritual experience. And man himself comes to know more and more clearly in this realm that in his own inner being he belongs to the spirit-world. He is aware of himself as a spirit among spirits, a member of the Primordial Spirits, and he will feel in his own self the word of the Primordial Spirit: 'I am the Primal Spirit.'

"If we now pass on to consider the cosmic aspects of the second region of Spirit-Land as described from the inner point of view of the soul, we shall find that this second region, the 'oceanic' region of Spirit-Land corresponds with the Jupiter region. Further, if we pass to the third region of Devachan, the 'Airy' region of Spirit-Land, we shall find that it corresponds with the influences of the Saturn region. What was described in *Theosophy* as the fourth region of Spirit-Land already extends beyond our planetary system. There the soul expands into still wider spaces, into the starry firmament itself. From the descriptions that were given from the inner standpoint of the soul, it will be quite clear to you that the experiences of the soul in the fourth region of Spirit-Land could not be undergone in any realm where the spatial relationship to the Earth is still the same as that of the planetary system. There is something so utterly foreign in what is conveyed by the fourth region of Spirit-Land that it can never correspond with what can be experienced even within the outermost planetary sphere, the Saturn sphere.

"Therefore, the soul passes into the starry firmament, that is to say into distances more and more remote both from the Earth and also from the Sun. These distant realms are described in the account of the three highest regions of Spirit-Land traversed by the soul before it begins to draw together again and to pass, in the reverse order, through all the preceding conditions. On this journey the soul acquires the forces by means of which it can build up a new life on Earth.

"In general, it can be said that when the soul has passed through the Sun region it has finished with every element of 'personality.' What is experienced beyond the Sun region, beyond the region of Soul-Life in the true sense, is spiritual; it transcends everything that is personal. What the soul then experiences as 'Thou art that'—and especially in our time as the Buddha-impulse in the Mars region—is something that seems strange here on Earth, though it is not so on Mars; it is the impulse denoted by the word 'Nirvana.' This means liberation from everything that is significant on the Earth, for the soul begins to realize the great cosmic significance of universal space. In living through all this, the soul emancipates itself entirely from the element of personality.

"In the Mars region, the lowest region of Spirit-Land, where the soul acquires understanding of the 'Thou art that', or, as we should put it today, receives the Buddha-impulse, it frees itself from everything that is earthly. After the soul has become inwardly free of this—and the Christ Impulse is needed here—it also liberates itself spiritually by recognizing that all ties of blood are forged on Earth and therefore belong by nature to the Earth. But the soul then passes on to new conditions.

"In the Jupiter region, conditions which force the soul into some particular creed are dissolved. We have heard that the soul can pass through the Mercury region with companionship only if it had adopted a creed; without religion in some form it would be lonely and isolated. We have also heard that the soul can pass through the Sun region only when it has learnt to understand the creeds of all religions on the Earth. In the Jupiter region, however, the soul must liberate itself entirely from the particular creed to which it belonged during life on Earth. This was not an essentially personal attachment;

but something into which it was born and was shared in the company with other souls.

"Thus, the soul can pass through the Mercury region only if it has acquired religious ideas in earthly life; it can pass through the Sun region only if it has developed some measure of understanding of all such beliefs. The soul can pass through the Jupiter region only if it is able to liberate itself from the particular confession to which it belonged on Earth; merely to understand the others is not enough. For during the passage through the Jupiter region, it will be decided whether in the next life the soul will have to be connected with the same creed as before, or whether it has experienced everything that can be offered by one particular creed. In the Mercury sphere the soul garners the fruits of a particular faith; in the Sun sphere the fruits of an understanding of all forms of religious life; but when it reaches the Jupiter region the soul must be able to lay the foundation for a new relationship to religion during the next life on Earth.

"These are three stages experienced by the soul between death and the new birth: first it experiences inwardly the fruits of the faith to which it belonged in the last life; then the fruits of having developed the capacity to appreciate the value of all other religious beliefs; and then it must free itself so completely from the beliefs held in the last life that it can wholeheartedly adopt a different religion. This cannot be achieved by attaching equal value to all creeds; and we know that on its return journey through these regions the soul comes once again into the Jupiter region and there prepares the traits enabling it to live in the fullest sense in a different religion in the next life. In this way the forces which the soul needs in order to shape a new life are gradually impressed into it."

The Mysteries of Sleep and Dreams

Even though humanity has placed the most profound attention and interest on discovering the nature of sleep and dreams, it has understood little and is still mystified by the mysteries found in the night. Sleep is considered the "little death" that informs both our waking and sleeping hours. About one third of human life is spent in sleep, and even though clever scientists have analyzed what they can from sleep and dreams though statistics and "measure, number, and weight", they ultimately admit they know almost nothing about the effects of "sufficient quality sleep" upon the psychological and spiritual nature of the human being. Without "good sleep", humans fall apart psychologically and can become rather useless in the "waking" world. The "cause and effect" of dreams leaves scientists baffled and promising new and further research on this oldest of human puzzles. The ancients had temples where people came to sleep and dream, and then have those dreams interpreted by the temple priests and priestesses. Usually, exposure to sunlight was the major cure for bad dreams and physical illness. Thus, modern science seems to know less about sleep and dreams than our ancestors did.

Novalis speaks of the mysteries of sleep in a most beautiful way:

"I turn away from the light to the holy, inexpressible, mysterious night. Light had its allotted time; but timeless and infinite is the reign of the night – the duration of sleep eternal. But even more heavenly than the flashing stars are those

infinite eyes which the night opens within us, and which see further even than the palest of those innumerable hosts."
Novalis, *Hymns to the Night*

"We dream of travels throughout the universe: is not the universe within us? We do not know the depths of our spirit. The mysterious path leads within. In us, or nowhere, lies eternity with its worlds, the past and the future."
Novalis, *Pollen and Fragments*

Prophetic dreams, visions, daydreams, and precognitive dreams fill the holy books of the different religions. Many of the prophets of the *Old Testament* were advisors to kings and rulers who guided their culture via the interpretation of the king's, or their own, dreams. The king dreamt for the entire kingdom; but often could not interpret the mysterious symbols and chaotic storylines of dreams. It took wisdom and insight to unravel what was meant in a dream. Dreams were seen to originate in the divine world, sent as messengers of the gods. But only a spiritual initiate could ferret out the hidden meaning of a dream's dynamic symbols. This gift of discernment was considered extremely important for creating a "bridge of communication" between the waking world and the ocean of messages arising in dreams.
The necessity to comprehend dreams is still paramount in human evolution. Dreams that arise from sleep or daydreams often become the driving force of one's personal destiny.

Science tells us that we have different stages of sleep that repeat themselves throughout, some with dreams and some without. They call these stages "rapid eye movement" or "non-rapid eye movement"; but, in effect, they don't know much more than that. They measure and label, but fall short of understanding the cause, nature, or mechanisms of these stages of sleep. They are able to measure brainwaves of various types and intensity; but again, can't understand what drives brain-wave phenomena. Science, limited to the five senses, can't make heads nor tails of what causes the various manifestations and effects of sleep and dreams, even though they measure the activity of the brain during sleep and follow the motion of energy moving from one part of the brain to another. Science doesn't seem to be able to manipulate dreams, even though there are hundreds of man-made chemicals that can dramatically effect sleep and sleeplessness. The ancients knew that a life without sleep creates illness and perhaps a shortened life.

A life without dreams is considered normal in our hyper-materialistic age and the restorative powers of sleep and dreams are hardly considered an issue for good psychological and physical health. Ultimately, sleep and dreams remain hidden in the darkness of night, the bosom of the goddess Nyx, the Great Mother of Sleep and Death. All things fall back into Mother Night, from whence they came—the dark unseen world. But modern materialistic thinkers simply ignore sleep and dreams as the antithesis of waking consciousness, which by them is much preferred. The waking condition of consciousness is seen as the ultimate, while all else is like common dust—dreams of fancy. This sad devolution of human consciousness sounds the death knell of soul and spiritual evolution and ignores the mercy and grace of life-giving sleep and dreams and the blessings of death.

Waking consciousness wears down the life body (etheric body) of the human being during the day. The physical and etheric bodies are worn out by the desire-body (astral body) and the "I Am" (ego) during the course of wakefulness. During sleep, the etheric body restores the physical body while the astral body and ego are, more or less, outside of the etheric and physical bodies. The intermittent awareness of the ego during sleep is attempting to digest and integrate the thinking, feeling, and willing of the human being that was expended during the waking hours. Thus, night-time heals daytime, or the human being cannot maintain homeostasis and equilibrium between these two entirely different worlds that are often quite the opposite. During sleep, reason and morality don't seem to rule in that realm, whereas they are key components of the waking world. The physical laws of space and time have but little authority in dreams. Thus, we have two distinct lives and they often do not coincide or agree, creating conundrums for the conscious, subconscious and the unconscious aspects of the waking mind to contemplate.

Rudolf Steiner, the great spiritual scientist, helps us understand the nature and mechanisms of sleep, dreams, and death. He also gives indications on the psychological, mental, and psycho-kinetic aspects of the stages of dreams. He clearly describes the differences between the sleep and dreams of materialists compared to spiritual scientists (aspirants and initiates). Steiner has given us far more information about sleep and dreams than all of modern materialistic science. These short quotes of Steiner demonstrate his insightfulness concerning these states of being. These short quotes can be found in a section below in their unedited form with citations.

Rudolf Steiner's Thoughts on Sleep and Dreams

"Sleep is a great educator."

"In deep sleep we experience unconsciously the spiritual aspect of our daily life."

"The existing destiny of a person confronts his soul during sleep."

"What rests in the depths of sleep was also the source of what preserved humanity's knowledge of the divine."

"During the sleep state, the astral body receives images from the world about it. It lives there in the universe, separated from the physical and ether bodies, in the same universe out of which the entire human being is born. The astral body, during sleep, returns to its home and on awaking brings back with it, renewed forces into life."

"Hence, during the whole of our existence on Earth, the experiences of the ego in sleep remain subconscious for ordinary consciousness, and even for Imaginative consciousness."

"Dreams take shape in order that certain tensions in the soul may be overcome."

"The world of dream-pictures is really like a veil concealing the spiritual world. When we dream, we sink down into this spiritual reality."

"In the life of dreams, the soul is in the world of the eternal, free from the body."

"In dreams, a person experiences the spiritual world in such a way that as the result of the impact with the bodily constitution, sense-images take shape."

"Dreams are a definite signpost to the spiritual world itself. The realm of dreams is an admonition to humanity to seek the spiritual world."

"Neither logic or moral judgment play any part at all in dreams. Dreams have a rule entirely different from that of ordinary logic. Moral judgment is silent in dreams."

"In sleep, we all live within the formative forces of the Cosmos, within the cosmic thoughts; just as man is immersed when he jumps into water, so is everyone immersed, in sleep, in the formative forces of the Cosmos."

"Our life of soul from going to sleep to waking is, so to say, in a little planetary Cosmos. Thus, during sleep man becomes, in very truth, a cosmic being."

"From the time I go to sleep until I awaken, my soul will be in the spirit world to meet the higher being who guides me through this Earthly life—the guiding genius of my life. When I awaken from this meeting, I will have felt the wafting of the wings of my genius that has touched my soul."

"When we cross the Threshold to the spiritual world, we are at once faced with three worlds. One might say that a person lives a philosophical life during the first stage of sleep, and in the second stage he lives a cosmological life, so, in the third stage, he lives a life of being permeated with divinity."

"Dreams arise when the soul impacts the body. The dream is not experienced in the body, but it is caused by the impact of the soul with the body."

"In dreams, the human being is not experiencing through the bodily constitution but through the spirit-and-soul."

"Dreams lead us to recognize that they are like a window into the super-sensible world. Behind this window the ego is actively weaving, and this weaving goes on from one earthly life to the next."

"The dreams we have as we go to sleep, and the dreams we have just before waking, both draw on the experiences of the day, break them up and give them all sorts of fantastic forms."

"In one kind of dream, we have pictures of experiences undergone in the outer world; in the other, pictorial representations of our own internal organs."

"The difference between dream-consciousness and the waking state grows ever smaller and smaller. The dreamer becomes, in the fullest meaning of the word, awake in his dreamlife. It must become possible for him during waking hours to recall quite consciously the beings he has observed in dreams."

"The dream therefore points to deep subconscious and unconscious grounds of the life of soul. But the pictures unfolded by the dream are only a clothing of what is actually being experienced in the course of it."

Nightly Inspiration

From the realm of night, the ancients received shared dreams, visions, and communications with higher worlds—sometimes called the realm of fairy, fantasy, visions, prophecy, dreams, and nightmares. Over long periods of time, individual tribes and kingdoms shared common dreams, fables, legends, myths, and spiritual insight that became a catechism of moral teachings. These stories are found in all traditional religions as fables, parables, and teachings that provide moral instruction and training. They often have cruel and violent elements to the stories and severe punishments for evildoers. Animals, as symbols of the human astral body, often play the lead characters in these moral imaginations and exemplify exaggerated desires, and then suffer the consequences for the evil deeds. The ancient Indian *Jataka Tales* or *Aesop's Fables*, or *Grimm's Fairy Tales* are "made of such things as dreams are made." These dream stories transcend space and time and directly encounter the divine moral world through the plot of the story and its outcome. Fairy tales take place in realms beyond space and time—"once upon a time", and "if things have not changed, they are still there today"- and create a realm beyond the limits of time and space that is transcendent. Through the catharsis of the characters in the story, the collective "group soul" instructs the individual about the path to moral development—a sort of moral collective unconsciousness rising into wakefulness. Some dreams and fairy tales are a Language of the Spirit that was taught to our ancestors from the "Imaginal Realm" as a moral path of spiritual development.

What are often called "dreams" in today's world are frequently confused with the "moral desires" of a person that arise from their personal hopes, visions, and longings for a beautiful future. These types of dreams, that can be the moral driving force throughout in entire life, are sometimes inspired by intuitions that arise in dreams, dreamless sleep, and trance states of consciousness during sleep. Once again, sleep delivers the teachings of the spiritual world, the moral world order that arises in a person through waking, dreaming, unconsciousness, and subconsciousness. Often, anyone but an aspirant on the road to initiation will not be able to tell whether their personal "dreams" for their life came from Day or Night consciousness, or a blend of the two. In other words, from sleep comes a dialogue with the divine, a transcendent experience in a realm other than the physical realm that seems to possess a higher moral consciousness, and a living conscience.

During sleep we contact another world, not a silly world of multiple dimensions, divergent timelines, alternate universes, or aliens from another galaxy; but, a world where our sacred, daily restoration takes place. For those who can "wake-up" in their dreams, dreamless sleep, and dreamless trance states of consciousness, it is a realm where you can meet and commune with higher hierarchical beings who live there. In the three realms of sleep and dreams, we may contact Angels through Moral Imagination created through "living light" that is filled with wisdom and warmth. Through interactions with Archangels, we may unite with Moral Inspiration that sounds through the solar system's harmony of the spheres. Through uniting with the Archai (Time Spirits), Moral Intuitions act with the spiritual power of knowing through the creative Divine Word—the force of eternal creation raying in from the fixed stars. These three realms are usually closed to those who haven't done the requisite preparation in moral training, mind control through refined thinking, and the development of a pure and stainless heart of selflessness.

Sleep is the 'little sister of death' and, essentially, they share the same realms. During sleep and during death, the soul and spirit (astral and ego) expand outwards into nine realms of being. Humans, at the current stage of evolution, only remember the first three generally; and even then, in a much-diminished replica of those realms. Materialists, who have no spiritual practice, cannot expand outward in all directions even to the realm of the Moon's sphere of activity. They are bound by their attachment to the material world and have developed no love for the spiritual beings who inhabit the higher realms. Thus, they can only rise to the lower levels of astral desire between the Earth and the Moon. This realm is sometimes referred to as the realm of hungry ghosts, who eat the un-satiated desire of unwitting humans. Asuric beings feed from the actions of the Seven Deadly Sins as nourishment while Ahriman instills evil during sleep to help imprison humans in the physical world.

An initiate, on the other hand, during sleep expands outwards through the first three realms of the Angels, Archangels, and Archai into the Sun realm (Christ) and the planetary spheres beyond: Mars, Jupiter, and Saturn. Reaching the "ring pass not", the rings of Saturn, the initiate looks out to the sphere of the fixed stars in all directions and receives the blessings of the higher hierarchies of the Thrones, Cherubim, and Seraphim. Then, the initiate turns and proceeds back thru all nine realms, including the Sun realm where the Kyriotetes, Dynamis, and Elohim work, into the lower stages of consciousness approaching the dream state again with the help of the Moon.

The path of the initiate at night is the same path taken after death. After death, there are a few more steps to be taken, but the nine realms are the same living realms of the spiritual hierarchies that an initiate can experience with developed supersensible organs that understand the Language of the Spirit spoken at each level. An initiate, through spiritual practices, can also cross the threshold between the physical and spiritual world consciously in prayer, meditation, and spiritual rituals. While the aspirant is unconscious in these realms because they have little moral offerings to give to the hierarchical realms and thus cannot, in turn, be fed by the higher beings of the hierarchies while they pass through those realms. An initiate offers moral thinking, feeling, and willing that has been consciously developed out of freedom and love through higher consciousness as food for the gods, and then the gods offer the nectar and ambrosia of heaven in return. This symbiotic, spiritual relationship happens every night in sleep, as well as between death and a new birth. Sleep is practice for death, and death is a birth into the spirit. For an initiate, every deed is an opportunity for selfless love to flow through them to others from an endless source of moral, divine truth, beauty, goodness, and love. Thus, the initiate can manifest the "threshold consciousness" that creates an opportunity to bring spirit into the physical world and moral human love into the spirit realms. This restorative nourishment of humanity, and the spiritual hierarchies, is the reason sleep can bring new life to the etheric body.

Materialistic science recognizes four "states" of sleep: Rapid Eye Movement (REM), and three Non-REM states (N1, N2, and N3). The state of REM happens at the beginning of the 90 minute cycles of sleep, and again between N2 and N3, and again before waking. The state of REM is when the sleeper dreams. Little is understood about these cycles or why dreams appear during REM.

Rudolf Steiner teaches, like most religions, that one should pray before sleep and review your day in reverse order with special emphasis on how your thinking, feeling, and willing affected others throughout the day. It is important to do this in reverse order, from evening back to the morning. One must "re-perceive" one's deeds with a concern for the karmic influences you created by your thoughts, feelings, and deeds. These three elements of reviewing of the day, to create a "clear conscience", happen in the three realms that Steiner describes in detail and are now called N1, N2, and N3. Rapid Eye Movement is directly connected to the recommended "review of the day" in reverse order. In other words, the aspirant is going through the Rapid Eye Movement memory that is part of decompression and integration into the whole being of thinking, feeling, and willing in these Non-REM states of N1, N2, and N3. These realms coincide with Steiner's indications and illuminates the soul/spirit reality that N1 is the realm of Imagination and digests the thinking of the day, N2 is where Inspiration digests daily feelings, and N3 is the realm of Intuition where willpower and deeds are digested and integrated into the soul/spirit of the individual.

If aspirants faithfully review the day, looking for the karmic influences that were created, then they help the spiritual hierarchies in those three realms of sleep to "pre-digest" the thinking, feeling, and willing of the day. Then, human participation in karma and destiny becomes consciously evident and the aspirant is free to commune with higher beings and receive the gifts they wish to bestow on a soul/spirit that is acknowledging the work of the Divine. The aspirant and initiate become spiritual helpers in the process of "Earthly and Cosmic Nutrition", what Rudolf Steiner calls the "etherization of the blood."

Rudolf Steiner has provided the most comprehensive understanding of sleep and dreams available. We have collected numerous quotations from Dr. Steiner's different lecture cycles to illuminate his indications on these important areas of study and we provide them below to help you in your studies. But before we offer these wisdom-filled insights, we would like to summarize what modern science has to say about sleep and dreams.

The Materialistic Scientific View of Sleep and Dreams

According to the current Earth-bound scientific understanding of sleep and dreams, sleep is divided into two broad types: Non-Rapid Eye Movement (non-REM or NREM) sleep, and Rapid Eye Movement (REM) sleep. Non-REM and REM sleep are so different that physiologists identify them as distinct behavioral states. Non-REM sleep occurs first and after a transitional period that is called slow-wave sleep or deep sleep. During this phase, body temperature and heart rate fall, and the brain uses less energy. REM sleep, also known as paradoxical sleep, represents a smaller portion of total sleep time. REM sleep is the main occasion for dreams (or nightmares), and is associated with desynchronized and fast brain waves, eye movements, loss of muscle tone, and suspension of homeostasis.

The sleep cycle of alternate NREM and REM sleep takes an average of 90 minutes, occurring 4-6 times in a good night's sleep. The American Academy of Sleep Medicine (AASM) divides NREM into three stages: N1, N2, and N3, the last of which is also called delta sleep or slow-wave sleep. The whole period normally proceeds in the order: REM—N1 → N2 → N3 → N2 → REM. REM sleep also occurs as a person returns to stage 2 or 1 from a deep sleep. There is a greater amount of deep sleep (stage N3) earlier in the night, while the proportion of REM sleep increases in the two cycles just before natural awakening.

Lack of sleep affects our memory and ability to think clearly, and sleep deprivation can lead to neurological dysfunction, such as mood swings and hallucinations. Those who do not get enough sleep are at higher risk of developing obesity and cardiovascular disease; furthermore, sleep difficulties are associated with adverse effects on well-being, functioning, and quality of life. Lack of or altered sleep can disrupt family life, well-being, and the ability to care for others or oneself. Each phase and stage of sleep includes variations in muscle tone, brain wave patterns, and eye movements. The period spent in each sleep stage develops and changes as we age, with the consistent trend being that amounts of sleep decreases as individuals age.

Transitions between sleep and waking states are orchestrated by multiple brain structures, which include: the hypothalamus controls onset of sleep, the hippocampus controls memory active during dreaming, the amygdala controls the emotion center active during dreaming, the thalamus prevents sensory signals from reaching the cortex, the reticular formation regulates the transition between sleep and wakefulness, and the pons helps initiate REM sleep.

Approximately 75% of sleep is spent in the NREM stages, with the majority spent in the N2 stage. The first REM period is short, and, as the night progresses, longer periods of REM and decreased time in deep sleep (NREM) occur.

Beta waves are the highest frequency, lowest amplitude while Alpha waves are seen during quiet/relaxed wakefulness. The first stage is the waking stage which depends on whether the eyes are open or closed. During eye-open wakefulness, Beta waves predominate. As individuals become drowsy and close their eyes, Alpha waves become the predominant pattern.

N1 (Stage 1)—Light Sleep produces Theta waves at a low voltage. This is the lightest stage of sleep and begins when more than 50% of the Alpha waves are replaced with low-amplitude mixed-frequency (LAMF) activity. Muscle tone is present in the skeletal muscle and breathing tends to occur at a regular rate. This stage lasts around 1 to 5 minutes, consisting of 5% of total sleep time.

N2 (Stage 2)—Deeper Sleep produces Sleep Spindles and K complexes. This stage represents deeper sleep as your heart rate and body temperature drop. It is characterized by the presence of Sleep Spindles, K-complexes, or both. Sleep spindles are brief, powerful bursts of neuronal firing in the superior temporal gyri, anterior cingulate, insular cortices, and thalamus inducing calcium influx into cortical pyramidal cells. This mechanism is believed to be integral to synaptic plasticity. Numerous studies suggest that Sleep Spindles play an important role in memory consolidation, specifically procedural and declarative memory. K-complexes are long Delta waves that last for approximately one second and are known to be the longest and most distinct of all brain waves. K-complexes have been shown to function in maintaining sleep and memory consolidation. Stage 2 sleep lasts around 25 minutes in the first cycle and lengthens with each successive cycle, eventually consisting of about 45% of total sleep. This stage of sleep is when teeth grinding occurs.

N3 (Stage 3)—Deepest Non-REM Sleep produces Delta waves with the lowest frequency and highest amplitude. N3 is also known as Slow-Wave Sleep (SWS). This is considered the deepest stage of sleep and is characterized by signals with much lower frequencies and higher amplitudes, known as Delta waves. This stage is the most difficult to awaken from, and, for some people, even loud noises will not awaken them. As people age, they tend to spend less time in this slow, Delta wave sleep and more time in stage N2 sleep. Although this stage has the greatest arousal threshold, if someone is awoken during this stage, they will have a transient phase of mental fogginess, known as sleep inertia. This is the stage when the body repairs and regrows tissues, builds bone and muscle and strengthens the immune system. This is also the stage when sleepwalking, night terrors, and bedwetting occurs. It constitutes approximately 25% of total sleep time.

Rapid Eye Movement- REM produces Beta waves that are similar to brain waves during wakefulness. REM is associated with dreaming and is not considered a restful sleep stage. While the EEG is similar to an awake individual, the skeletal muscles are atonic and without movement, except for the eyes and diaphragmatic breathing muscles, which remain active. However, the breathing rate becomes more erratic and irregular. This stage usually starts 90 minutes after you fall asleep, with each of your REM cycles getting longer throughout the night. The first period typically lasts 10 minutes, with the final one lasting up to an hour. It constitutes approximately 25% of total sleep time.

REM is associated with dreaming and irregular muscle movements as well as rapid movements of the eyes. During REM, a person is more difficult to arouse by sensory stimuli than during SWS (Slow-Wave Sleep; N3). People tend to awaken spontaneously in the morning during an episode of REM sleep. REM produces a loss of motor tone, increased brain oxygen use, increased and variable pulse and blood pressure, increased levels of acetylcholine. The brain is highly active throughout REM sleep, increasing brain metabolism by up to 20%.

The REM phase is also known as paradoxical sleep and sometimes desynchronized sleep or dreamy sleep, because of physiological similarities to waking states including rapid, low-voltage desynchronized brain waves. Electrical and chemical activity regulating this phase seems to originate in the brain stem and is characterized most notably by an abundance of the neurotransmitter acetylcholine, combined with a nearly complete absence of monoamine neurotransmitters histamine, serotonin, and norepinephrine. Experiences of REM sleep are not transferred to permanent memory due to absence of norepinephrine.

The transition to REM sleep brings marked physical changes, beginning with electrical bursts called "ponto-geniculo-occipital waves" (PGO waves) originating in the brain stem. Organisms in REM sleep suspend central homeostasis, allowing large fluctuations in respiration, thermoregulation and circulation which do not occur in any other modes of sleeping or waking. During REM, the body abruptly loses muscle tone, a state known as REM atonia.

The most pronounced physiological changes in sleep occur in the brain. The brain uses significantly less energy during sleep than it does when awake, especially during non-REM sleep. In areas with reduced activity, the brain restores its supply of adenosine triphosphate (ATP), the molecule used for short-term storage and transport of energy. In quiet waking, the brain is responsible for 20% of the body's energy use, thus this reduction has a noticeable effect on overall energy consumption. During slow-wave sleep (SWS), humans secrete bursts of growth hormone. All sleep, even during the day, is associated with the secretion of prolactin.

Key physiological methods for monitoring and measuring changes during sleep include electroencephalography (EEG) of brain waves, electrooculography (EOG) of eye movements, and electromyography (EMG) of skeletal muscle activity. Simultaneous collection of these measurements is called polysomnography and can be performed in a specialized sleep laboratory. Sleep researchers also use simplified electrocardiography (EKG) for cardiac activity and actigraphy for motor movements. The electrical activity seen on an EEG represents brain waves. The amplitude of EEG waves at a particular frequency corresponds to various points in the sleep-wake cycle, such as being asleep, being awake, or falling asleep. Alpha, beta, theta, gamma, and delta waves are all seen in the different stages of sleep. Each waveform maintains a different frequency and amplitude depending on the sleep state.

Sleep and Dreams According to Rudolf Steiner

All quotations below are from the works of Dr. Rudolf Steiner. The initial group of shorter quotes can be found in their complete form, along with citations, in the section below them. Just as the Steiner material quoted above constitutes a sort of *"Book of the Dead"* derived from Steiner's life work of Anthroposophy, so too the extensive quotations below constitute a "source book" of what to expect from dreams, explanations of where they come from and what they might mean for the inner life of the aspirant. The psychology of sleep, and thus also death, is in its infancy stage of development. Psychologists and doctors have created scientific methods of studying sleep and yet have no comprehensive philosophy of sleep and death. Considering all that sleep psychologists have deduced about the state of consciousness we call sleep, dreams, dreamless sleep, and trance – these realms of sleep and death might as well be planets in a different galaxy! But then again, the same psychologists who study the human soul cannot tell us what waking conscious is, where it comes from or how it might metamorphose in the future. In fact, perception of either the outer world or the inner world is still an infantile science that, like a baby, refuses to acknowledge that the realms of sleep and death are spiritual realms that cannot be weighed, measured, or given a number by a materialistic scientist in a laboratory.

Some people are sleeping and dreaming in the daytime and quite awake and active at night in their dreams. So when Master Chuang said, "Now I do not know whether I was then a man dreaming I was a butterfly, or whether I am now a butterfly, dreaming I am a man." Rudolf Steiner gives us a puzzling indication when he says that what we remember from one life to another is what we dream at night. This is why the stage of life review is one third of the life of a person, because we sleep (perhaps to dream) one third of our life and that is what we carry over to the after-life. This is most puzzling to most and few can understand the implications of this profound indication.

The importance of sleep for good health is well known; but the effects of dreaming or not dreaming is little understood, nor can it be "studied" very easily since these realms are mostly invisible and personally subjective. Many understand though, that dreams and night-time visions and revelations connect to higher spiritual beings in the non-material realms beyond the physical plane. Other planes exist simultaneously that pass right through us without our conscious knowledge. But for some sensitive people, and for clairvoyants, those worlds can be witnessed consciously. Dreams are as real as physical life. Dreams carry messages about karma and reincarnation and often give moral answers to our questions, whether consciously asked or not. Dreams can take us beyond our imaginations or inspire us for life from a single dream experience. Some dreams never go away or recur at different intervals over short or long periods of time. Dreams can be precognitive or prophetic and warn us of things to come. Thus, dreams can be timeless, spaceless, and can seemingly takes us to worlds beyond our imagined cognizance.

Master Chuang has placed the conundrum of sleep and dreams into a clear perspective when he said:

> "Life, then, is really a dream, and we human beings are like travelers floating down the eternal river of time, embarking at a certain point and disembarking again at another point in order to make room for others waiting below the river to come aboard. Half of the poetry of life would be gone, if we did not

feel that life was either a dream, or a voyage with transient travelers, or merely a stage in which the actors seldom realized that they were playing their parts."

The study of sleep and dreams, especially in your own life, is an important aspect of the path of spiritual development. Rudolf Steiner tells us about the nature of the invisible worlds and how we can awaken to them while we are asleep and while we are in a waking condition. Learning to cross the threshold into the spiritual world consciously is a critical step towards knowledge of the higher worlds. It behooves the aspirant of Spiritual Spirit to study sleep, dreams, death, and the life after death to learn the Language of the Spirit used by the angelic hierarchies who live there and are anxious for us to commune with them in a clear, wakeful consciousness. Dr. Steiner tells us in *Life between Death and Birth*:

> "When we have gone to sleep, and the sense-perceptions have been gradually paralyzed and the will-impulses have ceased to work, we experience in the first place an undifferentiated condition of soul, comparable with swimming—space is almost completely wiped out. The soul feels as if it were like a wave in a great sea. The experience of being forsaken and alone or sinking into an abyss, hovering over an abyss as it were, fills the soul. However, a general sense of time persists.
>
> "During the first stage of sleep, subject and object cannot at first be distinguished. Night brings, at a certain stage of sleep, anxiety. Into this anxiety must flow power man has gained from religious or similar experience on the day before, then a reviving and refreshing force streams into the organism for the new day that follows.
>
> "Inspired knowledge leads us to see how this inner life of night-time is connected with an unfolding of inner forces, comparable with the unfolding of the forces of breathing and of circulation and is a copy of the planetary movements of our

system. We are inserted into something which is a copy, so to speak in miniature, of our planetary Cosmos or rather of its movements. Our life of soul from going to sleep to waking is, so to say, in a little planetary Cosmos.

"Whoever enters in a right and living way into an experience of the Mystery of Golgotha will have Christ for his strong guide in the moment when his soul comes into the realm of anxiety during the time between going to sleep and waking.

"He now lives in the third stage of sleep in the constellations, or rather in copies of the constellations, of the fixed stars of the Zodiac. Thus, during sleep man becomes in very truth a cosmic being. When through Intuition we attain to a knowledge of the experience of the fixed stars, then we learn at the same time that the forces which lead man back again into the physical organism are Moon forces.

"The initiative man is able to carry in his powers of ideation, and of feeling, and thought during day-waking life is an after-effect of the experience of the fixed stars during the night, whilst the powers of combination he is able to carry in them, the powers of wisdom and cleverness, are an after-effect of the planetary experience. The experience of the fixed stars shoots into our life of day by way of the metabolism of food. The whole process of metabolism is fired by what we experience at night in connection with the stars. Nor would we be able to think intelligently unless we received into our breathing and blood-circulation during the day the after-effects of the planetary experience of the night.

"To be sure, we are not spread out into the entire planetary Cosmos, but we are of extraordinary size while expanding outwards, compared with our physical size in the daytime.

"It is a fact that, during the night, every human being first experiences an etheric preliminary state of cosmic anxiety and longing for the Divine, then a planetary state, as he feels the facsimiles of the planetary movements in his astral body, and he has the experience of the fixed stars in that he feels—or would feel if he were conscious—that he experiences his own soul-spiritual inner self as a facsimile of the heavens, of the fixed stars.

"It is the lunar forces which again and again return him, when he wakes, to his physical body. The Moon is connected in general with all that brings the human being from his spiritual life into the physical life.

"This shows you that, whereas the human being in the sleep state experiences as his inner nature merely facsimiles of the planetary world, the world of the fixed stars, he now passes through these worlds in their reality between death and a new birth. He passes through these worlds; they become his inner nature.

"That which leaves us during sleep and returns on awakening consist of the actualized judgments of our moral deeds. If I have accomplished a good deed during the day, its effect is reflected in my sleep-body within the spirit-soul substance that leaves me during sleep. My moral quality lives within this. And, when the human being passes through the Portal of Death, he takes with him his whole actualized moral evaluation.

"During the first stage of sleep, one is a purely spiritual being yearning for the Divine. In the second stage of sleep man experiences a reflection of the movements of the planets, and how, for one who has already a relation to the Mystery of Golgotha, Christ then appears, to be his Guide through the otherwise chaotic experiences that come to him while he is living his way through a kind of reproduction or copy of the life of the stars and the planets.

"Between falling asleep and awakening, man actually covers the whole cosmic existence beyond the Earth. We leave behind us our religious feeling and our moral feeling, we leave them behind with the physical and with the ether-body, and our soul and spirit live as an a-moral being during the time of sleep.

"We are living during this time in a world that has been irradiated by the light of the Sun. This means that the moral ordering of the world has gone out of the ether. Consequently, the Ahrimanic Being has access to the ether in which we find ourselves as soon as we fall asleep. And this Ahrimanic Being speaks to man while he is asleep. And what he says is most mischievous, for he is rightly called the father of lies; he makes good appear bad to the sleeping human being and bad good. Ahriman makes evil appear good.

"The man of olden time passed into the group-soul when he fell asleep; and when he awoke and returned to his physical and to his etheric body, he brought with him a strong feeling of belonging to his group.

"Inasmuch as the ego is well inside the sympathetic system and the astral body well inside the spinal system during sleep, man with respect to his sympathetic and his spinal nervous system is awake in his sleep and asleep in his waking life.

"During sleep, therefore, he enters right into the things that in waking life show him only their outer side. But it is only what is experienced by the astral organization, when outside the physical and etheric bodies, that can be brought back into the thoughts of the etheric body, not what is experienced out there by the ego. Hence, during the whole of our existence on Earth, the experiences of the ego in sleep remain subconscious for ordinary consciousness, and even for Imaginative consciousness. They are revealed only to Inspired consciousness.

"In sleep a man gathers up sufficient strength to imprint on the etheric body those experiences that can be put into thoughts. But during his life on Earth he lacks the power to deal with the wishes and desires which during sleep are experienced by the Ego in connection with earthly affairs—for these also are gone over during sleep. In our epoch, therefore, only the part of sleep-life that can be transformed into thoughts, imprinted in thoughts, passes over into the conscious waking life of earthly men; while the sleep-experiences of the ego lie hidden behind the veil of existence.

"Between waking and sleeping we are left to form our own opinions about ourselves. As I have sufficiently shown during these lectures, the spiritual content of the Cosmos takes the moral as its natural law, and what the Cosmos has to say about our true nature and our actions is experienced by the ego during sleep.

"Whereas by day you go through your experiences—leaving short sleeps aside—from morning to evening, during the night, in sleep, you live through these experiences backwards—from evening to morning. This is in order that we may experience whatever the spiritual Cosmos has to say about the way we have lived through the day.

"Just as thoughts and ideas are for the waking consciousness the clearest and most definite things of all, while feeling is darker and really a kind of dreaming, and willing the condition of the greatest insensibility—as it were a kind of sleep—so we have these three degrees of the sleeping consciousness. We have the sleep in which ordinary consciousness experiences the dream and a higher clairvoyant consciousness the cosmic thoughts; we have the second state of sleep which for the ordinary consciousness remains hidden—but so appears to the consciousness of Inspiration that everywhere the deeds of divine, spiritual beings are revealed; and we have the third state of sleep, which to Intuitional consciousness is life within the divine, spiritual beings themselves.

"True and genuine love for human beings during the waking state leads us, during sleep, to the bosom of the Archai. And there, while the ego is resting in the bosom of these Beings, karma or destiny is shaped. Karma is woven by the ego during the period of sleep with the help of the Archai.

"When that which we bring out of sleep into the body lights up as the voice of conscience, there is working, in this voice, all that has been bestowed by the Hierarchies of the Exusiai and Kyriotetes.

"From out of sleep, Exusiai, Dynamis, Kyriotetes bear as moral power into our bodily nature what we grasp in thoughts: Seraphim, Cherubim and Thrones bear this out into the Universe, so that our own moral forces become world-creative forces.

"At the first stage of clairvoyance, greater order enters into dreams; man sees marvelous forms and hears words that are pregnant with meaning. At the second stage of clairvoyance, dreams become precise and clear. To attain the third stage of Devachan, thought must be freed from bondage to the things of the physical world. Man can then live consciously in the world of thought, quite independently of the actual content of thought."

Selections from Rudolf Steiner's Works on Sleep

Spiritual Relationships in the Human Organism, The Experiences of Sleep and their Spiritual Background, **Stuttgart, October 9, 1922, GA 218**

"When a man goes to sleep, you know how in the moment of doing so, the consciousness, already growing vague and indistinct, is often confused by dreams. This dream world can, to begin with, help us very little indeed towards a knowledge of the life of the soul. For all we can know about dreams in daytime consciousness with the ordinary means of knowledge remains something that is quite external. Dreams are obviously not things upon which we can build in a sure and well-defined way, until we have a knowledge about sleep itself by some other means. He who truly acquires a knowledge of the condition of sleep knows very well that dreams are, in reality, misleading rather than enlightening. What the soul experiences in sleep it experiences unconsciously. But now, since I am going to place a picture of it before you, arising from Imaginative, Inspired and Intuitive Knowledge, I must portray it as if it were experienced consciously. I shall have to describe to you the experiences of the soul from going to sleep to waking as if they were experienced in consciousness. They are not consciously experienced; but what I will describe is nevertheless experienced by the soul, albeit without awareness.

"When we have gone to sleep, and the sense-perceptions have been gradually paralyzed and the will-impulses have ceased to work, we experience in the first place an undifferentiated condition of soul. In this undefined experience a strong sense of time is present; but, all feeling of space is almost completely wiped out. It is an experience that is comparable with swimming; we are, so to speak, moving about in a general, indefinite world-substance.

"One might say, the soul feels as if it were like a wave in a great sea, a wave that is organized within itself and yet feels itself surrounded on every hand by the sea and affected by the influences of the sea much as during the life of day the soul is affected by impressions of color, tone or warmth, perceiving them in a quite definite and differentiated manner. In the life of day, you feel yourself as a human being enclosed within your skin and having a definite position in space. In the moment that follows the going to sleep, you feel like a wave in a universal sea; you feel yourself now here, now there; as I said, the definite sense of space ceases. A general sense of time, however, persists.

"And now a still further experience is united with this one. A tremendous need for the support of the spiritual makes itself felt in the soul, a great need and longing to be united with the spiritual. In the universal sea in which one is swimming, one has, as it were, lost that feeling of security which comes from being in contact with the material things of the world of our waking hours. Hence one feels—one would feel, that is, if the condition were conscious—a deep yearning to be united with the divine and spiritual. And one may say too that this experience of movement in an undifferentiated world-substance carries with it the sense of being concealed and protected within divine-spiritual reality.

"During sleep one enters in an intensely real and living way into the undefined existence I have described; nor would he ever in the waking state come to a feeling of God, were it not that he has experienced the corresponding fact in the first stage of sleep. We owe to sleep something that has untold significance for our deep inner nature as human beings.

"But now this experience is united with another, namely, an experience of being forsaken and alone. It is like sinking into an abyss. If a man were to experience consciously this first stage of sleep without right preparation, he would in truth be exposed to great risk; for he would find it quite unbearable to lose in this way almost all sense of space and live merely in a general, universal feeling of time, to feel himself in this vague way merely a part of a universal sea of substance, where scarcely anything is distinguishable—where indeed the only thing one can distinguish is that one is a self within a universal world-existence. If consciousness were present, one would actually have the sensation of hovering over an abyss.

"In the past, power came to people with the impulses they received from the Mystery-Centers, and they were able to carry out of ordinary day life into the life of night, into the life of sleep, the strength to hold their own against the anxiety described above. The anxiety rose up out of the depths of the life of sleep. If a person was to have power to bring away with them out of this anxiety not general fatigue or exhaustion or the like, but instead a freshness of his whole organism, then he had to acquire that power on the previous day during the waking life.

"Such is the connection between day and night. Night brings, at a certain stage of sleep, anxiety. Into this anxiety must flow power man has gained from religious or similar experience on the day before; and when these two things come together and unite— the power remaining over from the day before and the new and original experience of the night—then a reviving and refreshing force streams into the organism for the new day that follows.

"The experience of the soul during sleep is not attached in any way to the senses, nevertheless it too is a well-defined inner life that can also be referred to something, in the same way that the inner life of day can be referred to the life of breathing and the life of circulation. Inspired Knowledge leads us to see how this inner life of night-time is connected with an unfolding of inner forces, comparable with the unfolding of the forces of breathing and of circulation and is a copy of the planetary movements of our system. Note well, I do not say that every night from going to sleep until waking we are ourselves within, or united with, the movements of the planets, but that we are inserted into something which is a copy, so to speak in miniature, of our planetary Cosmos or rather of its movements. Then we must say for the night-time: there revolves in us a copy of the movement of Mercury, of the movement of Venus, of the movement of Jupiter. Our life of soul from going to sleep to waking is, so to say, in a little planetary Cosmos.

"Whoever enters in a right and living way into an experience of the Mystery of Golgotha will have Christ for his strong guide in the moment when his soul comes into the realm of anxiety during the time between going to sleep and waking. Thus, the humanity of modern times has through the Christ-experience what an older humanity had from the Mysteries.

"Having lived during the second stage of sleep in the copy of the planetary movements, he now lives in the constellations, or rather in copies of the constellations, of the fixed stars of the Zodiac. This experience is a very real fact during the third stage of the life of man by night. He begins then also to experience the difference between the Sun as a planet and as a fixed star.

"During the second stage of sleep the Sun has actually, in this experience, planetary qualities; we learn to know the conspicuous and distinct relation in which it stands to the whole life of man on Earth. In the third stage we learn to know the Sun in its constellation in relation to the other constellations of the stars, for example, of the Zodiac.

"We owe it to the experience of the planets that our breathing process and circulatory process are, if I may so express it, 'enfired'; but in order for these processes to be permeated, as they need to be, with substance, in order that they may be continually carrying the means of nourishment to the whole of the organism, they require the stimulation that is given by the experience of the fixed stars. Thus, during sleep man becomes in very truth a cosmic being. This third stage of sleep is the deepest of all. When through

Intuition we attain to a knowledge of the experience of the fixed stars, then we learn at the same time that the forces which lead man back again into the physical organism are Moon forces. The deepest point is reached in the third stage of sleep, and we are then led back stage-by-stage by the Moon forces, which are always intimately connected with the bringing into the physical world of soul-and-spirit.

"It is a fact that the initiative man is able to carry in his powers of ideation, and of feeling, and thought during day-waking life is an after-effect of the experience of the fixed stars during the night; whilst the powers of combination he is able to carry in them, the powers of wisdom and cleverness, are an after-effect of the planetary experience. That which rays into the life of day from the Cosmos, coming from the experience of the night, is obliged however to enter by way of the body. The experience of the fixed stars shoots into our life of day by way of the metabolism of food. Our food would not enter our head in such a way as to enable us to unfold powers of initiative, were it not that the whole process of metabolism is fired by what we experience at night in connection with the stars. Nor would we be able to think intelligently unless we received into our breathing and blood-circulation during the day the after-effects of the planetary experience of the night.

"A true understanding of the human being is alone possible when we become conscious in the widest sense of the fact that man lives not only in his physical body within his skin—but in the whole world. This life in the whole world is concealed from ordinary consciousness only because it is very much dulled and dimmed for the waking life of day. At most we can say that in the general sensation and experience of light we have something of an after-working of our share in the being of a universal Cosmos.

And there are perhaps other feelings, very dull and dim, wherein man has something left between waking and going to sleep of that sense of being within the Cosmos. All such feelings, however, that are given to man remain silent within him by day in order that he may unfold his individual consciousness, in order that he may not be disturbed by whatever plays into his experience from the Cosmos. During the night the case is reversed. There man has a cosmic experience. True, it is a copy only; but it is a faithful copy, as I have indicated. By night man has, in reality, a cosmic experience and because he must pass through this cosmic experience, therefore is his day-consciousness darkened and paralyzed."

The Concealed Aspects of Human Existence and the Christ Impulse, The Hague, November 5, 1922, GA 218

"After the transition through dreams—as I intimated before—man passes, as regards the normal consciousness, into unconsciousness. But the reality of this unconscious state, as it manifests itself to the higher, supersensible knowledge, is that, directly after falling asleep, man enters into a sort of contourless existence. If he should realize his condition consciously, he would feel himself poured out into an etheric realm. He would feel himself outside of his body, not limited, however, but widely diffused; he would sense or observe his body as some object outside of himself. If this condition should become conscious, it would be filled, as regards man's soul nature, with a certain inner anxiety or uneasiness. He feels that he has lost the firm support of the body, as though he stood before an abyss.

"This objective element of a soul-spirit anxiety man experiences while he enters through the portal of sleep into the sleep state. But with the feeling of anxiety something else is connected: a feeling of deep longing for a Divine-Spiritual Reality that streams and weaves through the Cosmos.

"If sleep continues, something peculiar occurs; the soul exists as though split, as though split up into many souls. If the human being should experience this condition consciously—which only the modern initiate can completely behold—he would have the sensation of being many souls and consequently think that he had lost himself. Every one of these soul beings, which really are merely shadowy images of souls, represents something in which he has lost himself. Through the after-effects of a religious mood, the soul has sufficient strength to bear the sensation of being split.

"In order to possess health during the waking hours of the day, it is essential that we carry into our sleep life the feeling of our unity with the divine-spiritual Beings, in whose realm of activity we immerse the eternal kernel of our own being. And it is only by a right existence within a spirit-soul world between falling asleep and awakening that we can produce the right and health-bringing forces of a spirit-soul element, so necessary for our waking life.

"During this second stage of sleep, the human being acquires not a cosmic consciousness, but a cosmic experience in lieu of the ordinary physical consciousness. As stated before, only the initiate goes through this cosmic experience consciously, but everyone has this experience in the night between falling asleep and waking up. And in this second stage of sleep the human being is in such a state of life that his inner nature carries out imitations of the planetary movements of our solar system. During the day we experience ourselves in our physical body. When we speak of ourselves as physical human beings, we say that inside of us are our lungs, our heart, our stomach, our brain, etc. ... this constitutes our physical inner nature. In the second stage of sleep the movement of Venus, of Mercury, of the Sun, and of the Moon constitute our inner spirit-soul nature. This whole reciprocal action of the planetary movements of our solar system, we do not bear it directly within us, not the planetary movements themselves; but facsimiles, astral facsimiles of them then constitute our inner organism. To be sure, we are not spread out into the entire planetary Cosmos; but we are of extraordinary size, compared with our physical size in the daytime. We do not bear within us the real Venus each time that we are in the state of sleep; but a facsimile of its movement. In the second stage of sleep, between falling asleep and awakening, that which occurs in the spirit-soul part of our being consists of these circulations of the planetary movements in astral substance, just as our blood circulates through our physical organism during the day, stimulated by the movement of breathing. Thus, through the night we have circulating within us as our inner life, so to speak, a facsimile of our Cosmos.

"After this experience, we enter the third stage of sleep. In this third stage we have an additional experience—of course, the experiences of the preceding stage always remains and the experiences of the next stage are added thereto—in the third stage is included, what I should like to call the experience of the fixed stars. After experiencing the circulation of the planetary facsimiles, we actually experience the formations of the fixed stars, which in former times, for instance, were called the images of the Zodiac. And this experience is essential to the soul aspect of the human being because he must carry the after-effect of this experience with the fixed stars into his waking life in order to have the strength at all to control and vitalize his physical organism at all times through his soul.

"It is a fact that, during the night, every human being first experiences an etheric preliminary state of cosmic anxiety and longing for the Divine, then a planetary state, as he feels the facsimiles of the planetary movements in his astral body, and he has the experience of the fixed stars in that he feels—or would feel if he were conscious—that he experiences his own soul-spiritual inner self as a facsimile of the heavens, of the fixed stars.

"While all other planetary and fixed star forces actually draw the human being out of his physical body, it is the lunar forces which again and again return him, when he wakes, to his physical body. The Moon is connected in general with all that brings the human being from his spiritual life into the physical life. It, therefore, makes no difference—the physical constellation is not the thing to be considered, although a certain significance attaches thereto—whether we have to do with new Moon, full Moon, the first or last quarter of the Moon; in the spiritual world the Moon is always present. It is the lunar forces which lead the human being back into the physical world, into his physical body.

"This shows you that, whereas the human being in the sleep state experiences as his inner nature merely facsimiles of the planetary world, the world of the fixed stars, he now passes through these worlds in their reality between death and a new birth. He passes through these worlds; they become his inner nature. And it is always the lunar forces which bring us back to the Earth. They differ essentially from all other stellar forces in this respect, in that they bring us back to the Earth. In the sleep state they bring us back to the Earth; they bring us back also after we have experienced all that I have briefly described, in order to enter once more a life course on the Earth.

"But let us consider once again that which is there outside of the physical body, in the form of the astral body and ego organization, between falling asleep and awakening. It is not fabricated from physical bones and physical blood; it is a spirit-soul entity. But our whole moral intrinsic quality is woven into it. Just as we consist, when awake, of bones, blood, and nerves, so does that which leaves us during sleep and returns on awakening consist of the actualized judgments of our moral deeds. If I have accomplished a good deed during the day, its effect is reflected in my sleep body within the spirit-soul substance that leaves me during sleep. My moral quality lives within this. And, when the human being passes through the Portal of Death, he takes with him his whole actualized moral evaluation. It is a fact that, between birth and death in the Earthly life, the human being creates within himself a second being. This second human being, who leaves the body every night, is the result of our moral or immoral life, and we take it with us through the Portal of Death."

Planetary Spheres and their Influence on Man's Life on Earth and in the Spiritual Worlds, Lecture IV, *Life in the Spiritual Spheres and the Return to Earth*, London, November 12, 1922, GA 218

"When man passes from day-consciousness into sleep-consciousness—which is for the man of the present time unconsciousness—he is not in his physical body, nor in his etheric body. During sleep he is a purely spiritual being.

"You will remember how in sleep man goes out into the cosmic ether and feeling himself in the midst of a vast and vague unknown is at first overcome with anxiety and apprehension; then you will also remember how in this moment something awakens in the soul which one can call—borrowing the expression from conscious life—a yearning for the Divine. And we went on to speak of how in the second stage of sleep man experiences a reflection of the movements of the planets; and how, for one who has already a relation to the Mystery of Golgotha, Christ then appears, to be his Guide through the otherwise chaotic experiences that come to him while he is living his way through a kind of reproduction or copy of the life of the stars and the planets. For now comes the experience of the fixed stars. Man goes forth, from the planetary spheres—we mean of course the copy of the planetary spheres—and enters upon an experience of the constellations of the fixed stars. So that between falling asleep and awaking, man covers the whole cosmic existence beyond the Earth. I told you moreover that it is the forces of the Moon (the spiritual counterpart of what reveals itself to us in the various lunar phenomena) that bring man back again in the morning—or whenever he wakes up—bring him back into his physical and into his etheric body.

"And when we fall asleep and leave our physical and etheric bodies, then we take with us what we have acquired in this way during waking hours on Earth by beholding Nature; but strange as it may sound, we leave behind us our religious feeling and our moral feeling, we leave them behind with the physical and with the ether-body, and our soul and spirit live as an a-moral being during the time of sleep.

"This has an important consequence for us. We are living during this time in a world that has been irradiated by the light of the Sun. This means that the moral ordering of the world has gone out of the ether. Consequently, the Ahrimanic Being has access to the ether in which we find ourselves as soon as we fall asleep. And this Ahrimanic Being speaks to man while he is asleep. And what he says is most mischievous, for he is rightly called the father of lies; he makes good appear bad to the sleeping human being and bad good.

"In the case of a highly conscientious and devout man, who has a fine moral feeling, his moral sensibility enters so deeply into his soul that he takes it with him into sleep; with the result that he sleeps badly, believing as he does that, he has been guilty of many misdeeds. A bad man, on the other hand, whose moral sensibility is very little developed, will carry with him into sleep no such pangs of conscience,—and this will mean of course at the same time that he will have, spiritually speaking, an open ear for the whisperings of Ahriman who makes evil appear good.

"The enticement to evil to which man is exposed during sleep is, in truth, exceedingly great, and it can easily happen that in the morning he brings over with him from sleep terrible demonic forces of temptation. Only when he has come down again into his physical and etheric body, will a man who is not very good and upright begin to feel pricks of conscience,—not before. There is thus abundant possibility for man to fall a victim to Ahriman during the time of sleep.

"Yes, sleep is a great educator, more than you would think; on the one hand it educates man, it is true, in evil, as we have seen; but on the other hand, it educates him in democracy. The man of olden time passed into the group-soul when he fell asleep; and when he awoke and returned to his physical and to his etheric body, he brought with him a strong feeling of belonging to his group.

"Man, of course, carries in him all the time the part of his nature that is exposed in sleep at the present day to the temptations of demonic forces, he has it in him continuously. Only, when he is awake, he has to let it merge into the moral and religious consciousness. The religious side of man is given to him, as we saw, by the powers that live with him in his physical body, and the moral side by the powers that live with him in his ether-body."

Philosophy, Cosmology and Religion, The Soul's Experiences in Sleep, Dornach, September 10, 1922, GA 215

"For ordinary consciousness the phenomena of sleep appear as follows: sense perception begins to dim down, in the end it is entirely extinguished; the same also happens in the case of thinking, feeling and willing. Except for the transitional state when we are dreaming, man sinks into an unconscious condition. But what happens to the soul then—and this must be strongly emphasized—is something absolutely real. What remains unconscious to ordinary consciousness in this respect can be illuminated by imaginative, inspired and intuitive cognition. Therefore, I will describe for you the soul's experiences during sleep. At least sketchily, I will describe how imagination, inspiration and intuition can perceive what, for ordinary consciousness, is unconscious. I will outline the soul's experiences as if they were lived through consciously; for they are experienced consciously through higher cognition. It is not as if the soul were unconscious throughout the night; but what would otherwise have remained unconscious can be seen by means of imagination, inspiration, and intuition. Light can in this way be cast upon it so that it becomes visible. The following then comes into view.

"When man first enters into the state of sleep, the sense world around him ceases to exist for the soul. He goes into an inner experience that is undifferentiated, in a certain sense indefinite. The soul feels—I say feels but it does not feel; if it were conscious, it would feel—it feels enlarged as in a widespread fog. In this inward feeling and experiencing during this first stage of sleep subject and object cannot at first be distinguished. No separate phenomena and facts are distinguishable; it is a general sensing of a nebulous universality, which is sensed as one's own existence. But simultaneously there appears in the sleeping person what may be called a deep need to rest in the divine essence of the Cosmos. With this outflowing of experience into an undifferentiated condition is mixed an indefinite longing—one must use such a word after all—"to rest in God." As I said, I describe it as if the events experienced unconsciously, were passed through consciously. Thus, the external world of daytime, everything the soul receives through the senses, is swallowed up. All the stimuli through which the soul feels in the body are gone and, likewise, all the impulses by means of which the soul sends its will through the body are gone. The soul has at first a general, universal sensation accompanied by a longing for God.

"In this condition, which arises initially after falling asleep, dreams can intervene. They are either symbolic pictures of outer experiences, memory pictures, symbolic images of inner bodily conditions, and so on, or they are dreams in which certain true facts of the spiritual world can be intermingled without the ordinary dreamer being able to acquire a definite knowledge of what the dreams really contain. Even for one who views this condition of soul with imaginative cognition—for by means of it one can do this already—dreams do not throw light upon the inner facts, rather do they veil the real truth. For this truth, in relation to what is meant here, can only be perceived by a person, if, out of his own free will, he prepares himself in an appropriate manner through soul exercises such as have been described here. Only as a result of these soul exercises can a clear view of this first stage of sleep be attained.

"If you look with such cognitional faculties into this first stage of sleep, when you can divine it, it shows itself to be similar to, but not exactly the same as the unconscious experiences of earliest childhood. Indeed, if man were in a position to bring these experiences to consciousness and pour them into the concepts and ideas of ordinary consciousness, such as philosophy is occupied with, then these philosophical ideas would attain reality. The philosophy to which we should thus attain would be something real. So, it can also be said that in the first stage of every sleep man becomes an unconscious philosopher. He attains what in waking consciousness is cultivated in his soul as ideas, as dialectics and logical laws. If the flowing into the cosmic mists of the etheric world and the soul's longing to rest in God could be permeated with the experience of actuality, if man could bring these two soul experiences to consciousness and pour them into abstract philosophical ideas, then these ideas would come alive. Philosophy would then be as it was in Greece before Socrates, and in still earlier epochs of humanity. It would be an inwardly experienced reality.

"We have now learned to know two stages of man's unfolding: that of his earliest childhood, which, if brought to consciousness, would represent the reality of philosophical ideas and the experience of the first stage of sleep, which, as we have noted, is quite similar to the unconscious experience of childhood, and which, when brought to consciousness, could in the same way give a living experience of reality to a philosophy worked out during waking life. That describes the first, somewhat brief stages that a human being undergoes from the time of falling asleep to waking up.

"After the soul has been for a time in the state of sleep described above, another condition sets in. This second stage of sleep is such that instead of the experience of his own physical and etheric bodies, which he has when awake, man has a form of experience through which he feels inside himself the Cosmos that in daytime surrounds him. While in the first stage the soul experiences no clear distinction between subject and object, this difference now becomes increasingly meaningful except that during sleep man has come into the reverse condition from that of being awake. He now feels and experiences himself in the Cosmos and looks back on his physical and etheric organisms as upon an object. Just as he vaguely feels his organs—lungs, liver, heart, and so on—in day consciousness; now, in sleep, he experiences the cosmic content within himself—he himself becomes, as it were, Cosmos in his soul. Not as if he extended out into the whole Cosmos; rather, he experiences something like a reflection of the Cosmos within him.

"The first unconscious experience—which even so is wholly real—is, I might say, a fragmentation of this inner soul experience. The soul feels as if it were divided up into many separate parts of a manifoldness. It feels itself not as a unity but as a multiplicity; as if, when awake, we were to experience ourselves in the brain not as a homogeneous being but as a multiplicity of eyes, ears, lungs, liver and so on, and we were missing the sense of unity. Thus, during sleep, we experience, so to say, the cosmic ingredients without at first experiencing their unity. That brings about a condition of soul which, if we were conscious of it, we should have to describe as permeated by anxiety, even fear. The soul, however, really experiences the objective processes that cause this nightly anxiety, just as the organic processes of the physical and etheric organisms underlie what might be experienced here or there by the soul as anxiety coming from within. They are, in fact, fear-inspiring occurrences that the soul has to live through.

"In this stage of sleep, occurrences of waking life now reveal their effects. For modern man living after the Mystery of Golgotha there appear the after-effects of what he experiences in waking life as inner religious devotion to Christ and the

Mystery of Golgotha. The attention man gives to it, all reverence and worship that he develops for the Christ and that Mystery during his waking life, have after-effects in this second stage of sleep. It was otherwise for those who lived on Earth before the Mystery of Golgotha. They received from their religious leaders appropriate measures, religious functions to carry out, whose effects they could carry over into sleep and that worked there in such a way that this anxiety could gradually be overcome. For a person living after the Mystery of Golgotha his inner bond with Christ, his feeling of belonging to Him, the religious rituals directed to Christ Jesus, his whole relation to Him and his actual conduct in reference to this relationship, all this now works into the life of sleep and helps to overcome that anxiety which oppresses the soul.

"If, in daytime, we have developed a relation to the Christ, we actually meet His guiding power during this second stage of sleep. It is this guiding power of Christ through which we overcome the anxiety that oppresses the soul. Out of this anxiety there develops a cosmic relationship of the soul to the world. As a result of the development of this relationship; but in such a way that the soul experiences it as its inner life, the movements of the planetary system in our solar Cosmos stand before the soul. It does not expand out into the planetary world during sleep, but an inner replica of it lives in the soul. It actually experiences the planetary Cosmos in a replica. Even if what the soul experiences every night as a small, inner globe, a celestial globe, does not illuminate day consciousness, it does stream into the reality of daily life and continues on in the physical and etheric organizations in the systems of breathing and blood circulation, the whole rhythmic system, we find that these processes are accompanied by impulses and stimuli that live in the physical and the etheric body and work into waking life out of the inner planetary experience which the soul has in sleep. While we are awake, therefore, the planetary movements of our solar system pulse through our breathing and circulation as after-effects of sleep.

"During sleep—supersensible vision shows us that astral and ego organizations are outside the physical and etheric bodies—the planetary movements do not work directly. They are experienced by the soul outside the physical and etheric organisms. But within the sleeping physical body the impulses from the previous night echo and reverberate, the same impulses that have pulsated through breathing and circulation during the day. During the following night an after-effect of these impulses is present, and they are renewed the next morning as a consequence of what the soul experienced in the night as an inner replica of the planetary Cosmos.

"Now in addition to this cosmic experience during the second stage of sleep something else happens. The soul receives distinct impressions of all the relationships it has ever entertained with human souls in its various lives on Earth. We actually have within us, I might say, "markings" of all the relationships we have had with other human souls in successive Earth lives. They now appear before the soul in a certain pictorial form. Although unconsciously, the soul really experiences everything that has been good or bad in its dealings with other people. Likewise, it experiences its developing relationships with spiritual beings who dwell in the Cosmos and never live in a physical body, who always live in a super-sensible existence as opposed to the physical life of man. The human soul in sleep thus lives in a rich network of relations with those human souls with whom it has established such connections. These connections reappear, as does everything that has remained from them as after-effects of the right and wrong a person has done to others, the good and evil he may have caused. In short, the existing destiny of a person confronts his soul in this stage of sleep.

"What an older philosophy has called karma appears at this stage every night before man's soul. Since the planetary experiences continue to work as stimuli in the breathing and blood circulation, and thus in man's physical and etheric organizations, it is possible for someone capable of perceiving such things through inspired cognition to observe that this experience of repeated Earth lives also plays over into day consciousness, even though it is not directly present. It is clearly evident to inspired cognition, which perceives what the soul experiences, that repeated Earth lives are a fact, for to the view of inspiration they present themselves directly together with the relationships established at any time with other people. Man's development through repeated Earth lives presents itself because these relationships are beheld. One relationship points back to one certain Earth life, another points to another life, and so on. In this way, karma appears before man's eyes as an established fact.

"The experiences of the soul during sleep work in such a manner into day consciousness that man's general mood, making itself felt during the day in the form of a dull awareness of himself, depends on what we undergo in this second stage of sleep. Whether we feel happy or unhappy in our dimly perceived inner self, whether we feel lively or languid, is to a great extent the result of what is experienced in this stage of sleep. So, during this stage we find ourselves actually outside in the Cosmos, even though what we experience within the soul is a copy of the Cosmos; and what we experience of repeated Earth lives and karma appears before the soul as images and reflections. These replicas of the Cosmos and our destiny that stand before our soul contain what can be called man's inner existence in the Cosmos. If you are able to formulate in concepts and ideas what has been attained through inspired cognition by letting it stream back into ordinary consciousness, you arrive at a true cosmology that encompasses the whole of man. Such a cosmology then is an experienced cosmology. We can say that when this stage of sleep is consciously reflected back, man learns to recognize himself as a member of the cosmic order—a cosmic order that is expressed in a planetary sense, as a cosmic ordering of nature.

"But now, within this cosmic order, the moral world order arises. This is not as it is in Earth life, where on the one side we find the order of nature with its own systems of laws but lacking morality, and on the other side a moral world order experienced as far as earthly existence is concerned only in the soul. Instead, we have a unified world before us. What we experience as a planetary Cosmos is permeated and spiritually impregnated by a continuous stream of moral impulses. We live simultaneously in a natural and a moral Cosmos.

"You realize the full significance of these nightly events for waking life. So, we can say that what the soul experiences in the Cosmos between going to sleep and waking is more real and full of meaning for man's outward configuration than what confronts him by day; for the life functions of the physical and etheric bodies, as well as our own moral condition, are results of our cosmic experience during sleep.

"The third stage of sleep is characterized by a gradual transition from experiences within the planetary Cosmos to an experience of the world of the fixed stars, so that this world is experienced by the soul as a kind of reflection. Yet these are not reflections of those outer sense pictures of the constellations such as we have in waking life. Instead, the soul becomes familiar with those beings of whom it was said in earlier lectures that intuition recognizes as the spiritual beings corresponding to the stars. Here in the sense world in our physical consciousness we experience the physical sense pictures of the stars. When, as I have described, we penetrate the spiritual world with intuition, we recognize that the Sun and other fixed stars as perceived by ordinary sense perception are merely the reflected physical images of certain spiritual beings. The soul lives within these spiritual beings of the stars during the third stage of sleep. It feels after-images of the star constellations, that is to say, it feels the relationships that exist between the activities of the spiritual star-beings. The soul experiences such constellations.

"Ancient dreamlike science specifically described how the life of the fixed star constellations and Zodiac streamed into the soul. This is, after all, the main part of the soul's experience in sleep. In the sense world you arrive at a better correspondence to the single spiritual beings if you look at the constellations as a whole instead of gazing at single stars. In sleep, the soul, being free of the physical and etheric bodies, becomes so liberated that it confronts them both as objects, just as we usually have around us the objects of the external world as perceived by the senses. The soul really finds its way as a spiritual being into a Cosmos consisting of other spiritual beings. What it unconsciously goes through there, can be illuminated by intuitive knowledge. But the experiences there also have their after-effects in waking life; the general well-being, health, and vigor of the human body—not of the soul as in the first stage of sleep—are after-effects of what the soul experiences during the night among star-beings. Especially there comes before the soul, even if unconsciously, the whole event of birth in its broadest sense; that is, the way the soul enters a physical body through conception and embryonic life. Again, there comes before the soul how the body is abandoned in death and how man's spirit being passes into the soul-spiritual world.

"Every night, the truth concerning the events of birth and death really confront the soul. It is also an after-effect of the night-time experiences that man has a dim feeling during the day that birth and death by no means signify for human life only what they appear to be to sense observation. It is simply not true that a man with sound common sense could believe that birth and death are nothing but the events they appear to be in outer material life. Man in fact does not believe this; but it is not true to say that the reason for his disbelief is only because in his fantasy he imagines that he is an eternal being whose existence persists beyond death. No, man cannot believe it because of the picture experienced every night by the soul of how man enters Earth life from the spiritual world and withdraws again into the world of spirit. This picture streams into the soul by day and is experienced by it as a vague feeling about the world and human life.

"What appears during waking life as religious longing, as religious awareness, is an after-effect of the soul's experience among the stars. What I have just described is the stage of man's deepest sleep. In actual fact, it is out of his sleep that man derives the religious feelings of his waking life.

"Just as religious life can be founded today in knowledge by means of the experience resembling that of primordial humanity but permeated and formulated in intuitions by the fully developed consciousness; it can also be said that man can attain this religious knowledge if, through super-sensible intuition, he is able to perceive and illuminate the condition of deepest sleep. For what rests in the depths of sleep was also the source of what preserved man's knowledge of the Divine. Our day-consciousness is only a reflection of the potentialities for consciousness open to man. Likewise, what man bears within him as a natural religious feeling appears as a reflection of the glory and sublimity experienced by his soul, even if unconsciously, in the third stage of sleep. Man sinks into the life of sleep not only to renew his tired body, or to gain the stimuli from sleep that his breathing and circulation need, or to acquire from the spiritual world the other impulses he needs. What permeates him with religious feeling penetrates to the soul's surface, to the region of day-consciousness from the profound depths through which human soul-life streams during sleep.

"One might say that as man lives a philosophical life during the first stage of sleep, similar to that of earliest childhood—however paradoxical that sounds to present-day consciousness—and as in the second stage he lives a cosmological life, so, in the third stage, he lives a life of being permeated with divinity. From this third stage of sleep, man must then return to daytime consciousness.

"Having retraced the above-mentioned stages in backward sequence during the last stage of sleep, man returns again to waking consciousness. Since man's soul and spirit are outside his physical and etheric organizations in sleep, if this phenomenon of sleep is to be comprehended fully, intuitive knowledge must answer the question: Why is man drawn back into his physical and etheric bodies again? What impulse is at work there? If the intuitive perception of sleep is extended far enough, it is possible to recognize this impulse. As man cognizes these spiritual beings who correspond to the Sun or the constellations of the other fixed stars, he then recognizes that the impulse comes from the spiritual beings whose reflection in our physical world is the Moon. Indeed, the forces of the Moon permeate our whole Cosmos, and when, through intuition, we recognize not only the physical existence of the Moon but also her spiritual correlations, we find that these spiritual beings, who correspond to the physical Moon, are the entities who, in their working together, produce the impulses to bring us back into our physical and etheric bodies after we have reached the deepest stage of sleep. It is above all the Moon forces that connect man's astral and ego organization with his physical and etheric organisms.

"Every night, when out of the spiritual world the soul desires to re-enter its physical and etheric bodies, it must place itself within the streams of the Moon forces. It is of no concern here—that will be obvious to you—whether it be new or full Moon. For even when, as new Moon, the Moon is not visible to the senses, those forces are nevertheless active throughout the Cosmos that bring the soul back into the etheric and physical bodies from the spiritual worlds. They are active even though the Moon's phases appearing to the senses as half-Moon, full Moon, etc., are metamorphosed sense pictures that correspond to events in the soul being of the Moon; these, to be sure, have something to do with man's spirit and soul in the physical and etheric bodies. Indeed, the particular configuration in which man's soul-spiritual and physical-etheric natures are linked is determined by those forces that rule and interweave in the Cosmos and come to physical expression in the Moon, the sense object, with her various phases that we perceive.

"Thus, we can also look into the concealed aspects of man's life of waking and sleeping and inform ourselves concerning what it is that brings him back each morning into his daytime life. He returns through the same stages in reverse order, and while he passes through the last stage, which is permeated by a longing for God, the dreams mix again into his sleep life, and he gradually submerges into his physical and etheric organizations."

The Cyclic Movement of Sleeping and Waking, Dornach, November 6, 1916, GA 172

"In waking life, we say: the Ego and astral body are inside the physical body and the etheric, in sleep they are outside. In general, it is so: sleeping and waking represent a kind of cyclic movement for the human being. Strictly speaking, it only applies to the head when we say that the Ego and astral body of man are outside the physical and etheric body during sleep. In actual fact, precisely because they are outside the physical and etheric head of man, the Ego and astral body in sleep are acting all the more vividly upon the rest of man's organization. During sleep—when the Ego and astral body are working- upon man as it were from without—all that is not 'head' in man, but the remainder of his organization, is subjected to a far stronger influence by the Ego and the astral body, than it is in waking life. Indeed, we may truly say, the influence which the Ego and astral body wield over the head of man in waking life—this influence they wield over the remaining organism during sleep.

"Bearing this in mind, we shall readily conceive that there is a peculiarly vivid relationship in sleep between our Ego and our sympathetic nervous system. This system, as you know, is mainly spread out in the abdominal organism, and with its strands it envelopes the spinal column from without. Now these relations between the Ego and the sympathetic system are loosened during our day-waking life. They are still there, but they are loosened. In sleep they are more intimate. Moreover, the relations between the astral body and nerves of the spinal column are more intimate in sleep than in our day-waking life. Thus, we may say: during our sleep the most intimate relationships arise, between our astral body and the nerves of our spinal column, and at the same time between our Ego and our sympathetic nervous system. In sleep, with our Ego we live more or less intensely in connection with our sympathetic system. Once the mysterious world of dreams is more accurately studied, what I am now saying out of spiritual-scientific research will soon be recognized.

"If you bear this in mind, you will find the way over to another most essential thought. Something deeply significant is given to our life inasmuch as there is this rhythmic alternation; for example, in the living-together of the Ego with the sympathetic [nervous system] and the astral body with the spinal nervous system-a rhythmic alternation which is really identical with that between sleeping and waking. It will not appear altogether surprising to you, if we now assert: Inasmuch as the Ego is well inside the sympathetic nervous system and the astral body well inside the spinal nervous system during sleep – man with respect to his sympathetic nervous system, and his spinal nervous system, is awake in his sleep and asleep in his waking life.

"Man needs this rhythmic alternation. His Ego and his astral body are in the head during his day-waking life and outside of it during his sleep. Inasmuch as they are outside the head during sleep, they develop a vivid inner life together with this other system, as I described before. The Ego and astral body need this alternation of diving down into the head and going out of it. When man is outside the head with his Ego and his astral body, he develops not only the intimate relation to the rest of the body through the sympathetic nervous system and the spinal nervous system. For on the other side, he also develops spiritual relations to the Spiritual World. Corresponding to this active living-together with the spinal nervous system and with the sympathetic nervous system, we have an active living-together in soul and spirit with the Spiritual World. At night the soul-and-spirit is outside the head, and consequently unfolds this vivid life in the remaining organism. Conversely, we must say that in the day-waking life, when the Ego and astral body are more in the head, we are living together spiritually with our surrounding spiritual environment. We dive down, as it were, into a spiritual inner world in our sleep; but on awakening we plunge into a spiritual world around us."

Rudolf Steiner on the Process of Sleep

An entire psychology of sleep could be constructed from what Rudolf Steiner presented in his seminal work, *An Outline of Occult Science*. To explain the nature of sleep and what happens to the human physical body, etheric body, astral body, and ego at night requires a comprehensive understanding of the terms and language of theosophy and anthroposophy to derive this "new psychology of sleep" found in Dr. Steiner's work. The modern materialistic scientist is trying to study the invisible world of sleep and dreams and yet denies the existence of the invisible life body (etheric body) that builds and sustains the human physical body. Then, to add to the confusion of the godless scientist, Dr. Steiner informs us that the astral body, or body of desires, separate along with the "I Am" (or ego)—and leave the etheric body and physical body lying on the bed while we are asleep. For due to their supersensible nature—the ego, astral body and etheric body can't even be seen by the materialistic scientist! To further challenge the sense-bound materialistic scientist, Steiner also categorizes the soul into three parts: Sentient Soul, Intellectual Soul, and Consciousness Soul. These three soul capacities, in turn, are linked to the trinitarian (3x3) ninefold human constitution as presented by Dr. Steiner. While our modern materialistic scientist; whether he be a psychiatrist, a psychologist or other various disciplines—due to his lack of supersensible faculties of perception—would not only deny the existence of most of the ninefold constitution of the human being but would probably consider someone psychologically "imbalanced" and living in "magical thinking" who believed the human being could have so many "invisible parts."

Nonetheless, in light of the foregoing observations, keep in mind that Dr. Steiner's explanations of the stages of sleep coincide precisely with the observed data about sleep that machines and sleep specialists have measured and codified; and yet, based as they are on a materialistic worldview, sleep psychologists haven't a clue about what the data means or how it can help those restless souls in need of a good night's sleep! Consequently, there are virtually hundreds of drugs and therapies used to induce sleep and stop the symptoms of sleeplessness and insomnia. Unfortunately, drug induced sleep often does not leave the person feeling refreshed in the morning; and often leads to a gray world of pseudo-wakefulness during the day as a result of these sleep drugs or treatments.

Sleep is the great universal panacea that cannot be replaced and has a profound effect upon the health and well-being of the individual. For the sincere seeker described by Wolfram von Eschenbach in his epic poem Parzival strives to be blameless and "free from all thought of guile" like the maiden Antikonie:

> "Now hearken to me and heed me, as with gracious words I'd greet Antikonie, free from falsehood, a maiden pure and sweet. In such wise did she ever bear her that never a doubting word, Were one fain to sing her praises, from the lips of men was heard; For no heart but wished her gladness, and no mouth but spake her free from all thought of guile -Far-reaching, as a falcon's eye can see, Shone the light of her gracious presence, as the light of a balsam rare that burneth, and sheddeth perfume, and sweeteneth the scented air. And her will was ever gracious, as the will of a maid should be, And she spake to her royal brother of a true heart right maidenly."
>
> *Parzival*, Book VIII (verses 497-506; translator: Jessie L. Weston)

In keeping with this spirit of the quest, the fruit of the sincere seeker striving to maintain the proper mood of soul during their waking state, is that the realm of sleep gradually becomes transformed through the Grace of Christ by the realms of the Celestial Hierarchies that serve the Christ into a restorative sanctuary—where their soul and spirit can meet and dance throughout the night within the shimmering worlds of light and the sounding of the heavenly "Music of the Spheres."

> "Whenever a human being has reached the degree of maturity that renders him worthy of being chosen by the Holy Grail, his name will appear on the sacred vessel, and the call will then find him wherever he may be. Kundry, the messenger of the Holy Grail, will come to meet him, will summon him and will guide him to the secret place that through no effort of his own he could ever have reached."
>
> "The word 'Grail' is connected with the Latin word 'gradalis' from which again is derived the English word 'gradual.' Only 'gradually', through strictly determined stages of inner development can we hope to come nearer to the mystery. The whole of the sublime truth is available indeed—everywhere and at all times—but our own nature obscures it and breaks it into fragments. Answers to our questions will often be given to us, but our own immaturity may prevent us from recognizing them. Now we can even begin to be grateful for the fact that the truth is so difficult to assess. The very efforts we have to make towards finding it help us to transform ourselves and to acquire the necessary degree of inner maturity. The moment we have—through our own efforts—achieved the inner victory, the outer realities of life tune in on it and, as if by magic, the truth reveals itself."
>
> Ursula Grahl, "In Quest of the Holy Grail", Golden Blade, No. 33, 1981 (pg. 36)

Furthermore, if the soul brings virtue as nourishment to the spiritual world during sleep, then the realm of sleep gives heavenly nourishment to the soul in return. In the "Language of the Birds", that is what is meant by "the feast of the Grail." For we feed the spiritual world in sleep, and the spiritual world feeds us, in turn, for the challenges of the next day. Likewise, without this reciprocal relationship of human and cosmic nourishment, one's health and sense of well-being become compromised. Let's hear what Rudolf Steiner had to say in his monumental work, *Occult Science* about the nature and importance of sleep and death and the worlds we share with the Celestial Hierarchies that serve the Christ during sleep and after death.

Occult Science, Section III *Sleep and Death*, GA 13

"When man sinks into sleep, there is a change in the relationship of his members. That part of the sleeping man that lies in bed contains the physical and ether bodies, but not the astral body and not the ego. Because the ether body remains united with the physical body in sleep, the life-activities continue; for, the moment the physical body were left to itself, it would have to crumble to dust. What, however, is extinguished in sleep includes the mental images, pain and pleasure, joy and sorrow, the capacity to express a conscious will, and similar facts of existence. The astral body is the bearer of all this. An unbiased point-of-view can naturally never entertain the thought that in sleep the astral body is destroyed along with all pleasure and pain and the world of ideas and will. It simply exists in another state. In order that the human ego and astral body not only be filled with joy and sorrow and all the other facts of existence mentioned above, but also have a conscious perception of them, it is necessary that the astral body be united with the physical and ether bodies. In the waking state, all three are united; in the sleeping state, the astral body withdraws from the physical and ether bodies. It assumes a different kind of existence from the one that falls to its lot during its union with the physical and ether bodies. It is the task of supersensible knowledge to consider this other kind of existence in the astral body. Observed from the standpoint of the outer world, the astral body disappears in sleep; supersensible perception must follow its life until it again takes possession of the physical and ether bodies on awakening. Just as in all cases where it is a matter of knowledge of the hidden things and events of the world, so supersensible observation is necessary for the discovery of the facts of the sleeping state in their particular form.

"Although the astral body, during sleep, experiences no mental pictures and also no pleasure and pain, it does not remain inactive. On the contrary, it is just in the sleep state that a lively activity is incumbent upon it. It is an activity into which it must again and again enter in rhythmical succession, if it has been for a time active in connection with the physical and ether bodies. But this fatigue is the expression of the fact that the astral body and ego, during sleep, prepare themselves to transform, during the following waking state, what has arisen in the physical and ether bodies through purely organic formative activity when freed from the presence of the spirit and soul elements.

"Something similar occurs with the human astral body on awaking. During sleep it is in a world like itself; in a certain sense it constitutes something that belongs to this world. On awaking, the physical and ether bodies suck it up; they fill themselves with it. They contain the organs through which the astral body perceives the outer world. But in order that it may acquire this perception, it must separate itself from its own world. From this world it can only receive the prototypes that it needs for the ether body.—Just as the physical body receives its food, for example, from its environment, so during the sleep state the astral body receives images from the world about it. It lives there actually in the universe, separated from the physical and ether bodies, in the same universe out of which the entire human being is born. The source of the images through which the human being receives his form lies in this universe. During sleep he is harmoniously inserted into it, and during the waking state he lifts himself out of this all-encompassing harmony in order to gain external perception. In sleep, his astral body returns to this cosmic harmony and on awaking again brings back to his bodies sufficient strength from it to enable him to dispense with his dwelling within the cosmic harmony for a certain length of time. The astral body, during sleep, returns to its home and on awaking brings back with it renewed forces into life. These forces that the astral body brings with it on awaking find outer expression in the refreshment that healthy sleep affords. Further descriptions of occult science will show that this home of the astral body is more encompassing than that which belongs to the physical body of the physical environment in the narrower sense. Whereas the human being is physically a part of the Earth, his astral body belongs to worlds in which still other cosmic bodies besides our Earth are embedded. Therefore, he enters, during sleep, into a world to which other worlds than the Earth belong, a fact that will only become clear from later descriptions.

"We see that as soon as the senses cease their activity, something creative asserts itself in man. This is the same creative element that is also present in completely dreamless sleep and there presents the soul state that appears as the antithesis of the soul's waking state. If this dreamless sleep is to take place, the astral body must be withdrawn from the etheric and physical bodies. During the dream state, it is separated from the physical body in so far as it no longer has any connection with this body's sense organs; but. it still retains a certain connection with the ether body. That the processes of the astral body can be perceived in pictures is due to this connection with the ether body. The moment this connection ceases, the pictures sink down into the darkness of unconsciousness, and we have dreamless sleep. The arbitrary and often absurd character of dream pictures rests upon the fact that the astral body, because of its separation from the sense organs of the physical body, cannot relate its pictures to the proper objects and events of the external environment.

"In passing over into sleep, the astral body only severs its connection with the etheric and physical bodies, the latter remaining bound together; in death, the physical body, however, is severed from the etheric body. The physical body is left to its own forces and must, for that reason, disintegrate as a corpse. When death occurs, the etheric body enters into a state that it never experienced during the time between birth and death, except under rare conditions that will be spoken of later. It is now united with its astral body, without the presence of the physical body; for the etheric body and astral body do not separate immediately after death. For a time, they remain together by means of a force whose existence is easily understood. If it did not exist, the etheric body could not sever itself from the physical body; for it is bound to it. This is seen in sleep when the astral body is unable to tear these two members of the human organism apart. This force begins its activity at death. It severs the etheric body from the physical, with the result that the ether body is now united with the astral body. Supersensible observation shows that after death this union varies in different people. Its duration is measured by days. For the present this duration is only mentioned by way of information. Later the astral body separates from its ether body also and continues on its way bereft of it. During the union of the two bodies man is in a condition that enables him to perceive the experiences of his astral body. As long as the physical body is present, the work of refreshing the worn-out organs must begin from the moment the astral body is severed from it. With the severance of the physical body this work ceases. The force that is employed for this work when the human being sleeps remains after death and can now be used to make the astral body's own processes perceptible.

"In the period immediately following death the experiences of the past appear summarized in a memory-picture. After the separation of the etheric body and the astral body, the latter is left to itself in its further journey. It is not difficult to see that, within the astral body, everything remains that it has made its own through its own activity during its sojourn in the physical body. To a certain degree, the ego has developed Spirit-Self, Life-Spirit, and Spirit-Man. As far as they are developed, they receive their existence, not from what exists as organs in the bodies—but from the ego. The ego is the very member that needs no external organs for self-perception; it also needs none in order to remain in possession of what it has united with itself. The objection can be made, 'Why, then, is there no perception in sleep of this Spirit-Self, Life-Spirit, and Spirit-Man, which have been developed?' There is none because the ego is fettered to the physical body between birth and death. Even though in sleep the ego, united with the astral body, is outside the physical body, it remains, nevertheless, in close union with the latter; for the activity of the astral body is directed toward this physical body. Thus, the ego with its perception is relegated to the external sense world and cannot therefore receive the revelations of the spirit in its direct form."

The Evolution of Consciousness, During Sleep and Death, Penmaenmawr, August 26, 1923, GA 227

"If we have here the etheric body and the astral is there asleep, then on the verge of waking or of going to sleep a continuous struggle takes place, a movement full of life, expressed outwardly in the dream; but signifying inwardly this weaving of experiences into the etheric and physical bodies. It is only when a man has slept on some experience two or three times—perhaps more often—that the experience is united with the memories already bound up with his etheric and physical bodies. The point is that the experience has to be transformed into memory, which is left lying in bed during sleep; for a memory is essentially the expression in thought of the physical and etheric bodies.

"During sleep, a man lives with his Ego and astral organization outside his physical and etheric bodies. While in this state as a being of soul and spirit, as Ego and astral organization, he is interwoven with the spiritual forces pervading the whole Cosmos. He is *in the world* that is, figuratively speaking, *outside his skin*—the world of which the only impressions he receives in waking life come through his senses. During sleep, therefore, he enters right into the things that in waking life show him only their outer side. But it is only what is experienced by the astral organization, when outside the physical and etheric bodies, that can be brought back into the thoughts of the etheric body, not what is experienced out there by the Ego. Hence, during the whole of our existence on Earth, the experiences of the Ego in sleep remain subconscious for ordinary consciousness, and even for Imaginative consciousness. They are revealed only to Inspired consciousness, as already described.

"In sleep a man gathers up sufficient strength to imprint on the etheric body those experiences that can be put into thoughts.

But during his life on Earth, he lacks the power to deal with the wishes and desires which during sleep are experienced by the Ego in connection with earthly affairs—for these also are gone over during sleep. In our epoch, therefore, only the part of sleep-life that can be transformed into thoughts, imprinted in thoughts, passes over into the conscious waking life of earthly men, while the sleep-experiences of the Ego lie hidden behind the veil of existence.

"Now if we would pass on to the world accessible to Inspiration, in which we are as Ego between going to sleep and waking, we come to one dimension only; we then have to do with a one-dimensional world. This transition to a one-dimensional world, taken for granted by the faculty of Inspiration—the faculty, that is, of actually perceiving the spiritual in which we live between going to sleep and waking—this understanding of a world with only one dimension has always been part of Initiation-knowledge.

"But it is not only a human being himself who has something to say about his experiences; his experiences and actions are the concern of the whole Spiritual Cosmos. The Cosmos judges whether an action, a thought or feeling is to be declared good or bad. Between waking and sleeping we are left to form our own opinions about ourselves. As I have sufficiently shown during these lectures, the spiritual content of the Cosmos takes the moral as its natural law, and what the Cosmos has to say about our true nature and our actions is experienced by the Ego during sleep. Inspired cognition shows how the Ego, even during the shortest sleep, experiences over again everything the individual has gone through from his last moment of waking until his present sleep—however long or short this period may be. So a man, in the successive states of waking, sleeping, waking, sleeping, experiences again in sleep whatever he went through during his last waking time, especially where his own activities were concerned.

"As far as this is the experience of the Ego, it remains outside ordinary consciousness; but Inspiration can call it up. Then the particular nature of the experience is disclosed, and we find it is gone through in reverse order to our experience by day. Whereas by day you go through your experiences—leaving short sleeps aside—from morning to evening, during the night, in sleep, you live through these experiences backwards—from evening to morning. This is in order that we may experience whatever the spiritual Cosmos has to say about the way we have lived through the day.

"In fact, it is like this with the panorama that appears during those two or three days after death. Then, later, comes a period when soul and spirit have gained sufficient strength to experience in the spiritual world all that could manifest only unconsciously, in picture form, while we were asleep at night during our life on Earth. It now comes before us as experience. A man then passes through a period—lasting about one-third of his life on Earth, approximately the time normally spent in sleep—when he experiences his nights again, but in a backward direction. So, he lives through his last night first, then the night before, and so on right back to the time of his birth and conception."

***The Sun-Mystery and the Mystery of Death and Resurrection*, III —*The Three Stages of Sleep*, Dornach March 24, 1922, GA 211**

thoughts: we all live within these formative forces of the Cosmos, within the cosmic thoughts; just as man is immersed when he jumps into water, so is everyone immersed, in sleep, in the formative forces of the Cosmos. Besides this life within the formative forces of the Cosmos there are two other conditions of the life of sleep, just as in waking life the human being not only thinks but feels and wills. Thinking, the possession of thoughts, corresponds in sleep to the life of the cosmic formative forces. This means that, when we become conscious in the lightest sleep, we are living in the formative forces of the Cosmos. It is as though we were swimming through the Cosmos from one end to the other, floating through thoughts—thoughts which are, however, forces. In this lightest sleep we float through the thought-forces of the Cosmos. But there is also a deeper sleep—a sleep from which nothing can be brought into the waking life of the day unless we have practiced special exercises of the soul. A person can bring back something into the waking life through the dream only from the lightest sleep; but, as I have already said, these dream-pictures are not authoritative—for the same dream can be clothed in the most varied pictures. In very light sleep we can always dream, that is, we can always bring something over into consciousness; we can feel that we have had at least some experiences in sleep. This is, however, only the case with the very lightest kind of sleep. Of deeper sleep nothing can be known until we can enter it with Inspirational consciousness, and then we become aware of more than is described in *Occult Science*.

"When sleep is so light that dreams can be brought back into ordinary life, then one who is able to look into these worlds perceives the surging, weaving thought-pictures, the cosmic Imaginations which reveal cosmic mysteries showing that human beings indeed belong to a cosmic world just as they belong to the world in which they live consciously from awakening to falling asleep. For what I have described in *Occult Science* is not as though one merely painted something on a surface; but everything is in perpetual movement, in perpetual activity. At a definite moment, however, pictures begin to appear in this world through which human beings pass in light sleep, though they know nothing of it. The pictures become distinct, their light is enhanced; they reveal certain realities lying behind them. The pictures fade away again, and nothing remains in the consciousness but a kind of feeling that they have died down. Then they rise up again, and in this alternation of activity and withdrawal, something appears which can be called the harmony of the spheres, cosmic music. Thus, cosmic music does not reveal itself only as melody and harmony; but as the deeds and activities of those beings who dwell in the spiritual world, as the deeds of the Angels, Archangels, Archai, and so on.

"The spiritual beings who guide and direct the world out of the spirit are seen, moving, as it were, through the surging sea of pictures. It is the world that is perceived through Inspiration, the second world. Let me call it the revelations of spiritual cosmic beings. And this world of the revelation of spiritual cosmic beings is the *second element of sleep*, as feeling is the second element of waking consciousness. Thus during sleep, not only does the human being enter the realm of cosmic thoughts; but within these flowing cosmic thoughts there are revealed the deeds of cosmic beings who belong to the spiritual world.

"In addition to these two conditions of sleep there is yet a third of which human beings have as a rule *no sort of awareness*. They usually know that they can sleep lightly, and they know also that dreams emerge from this light sleep. They know that there is a dreamless sleep. But the utmost that they can know of this *third condition of sleep* is that on awakening they may be conscious of the fact that, during sleep, they had been faced with some difficulty, with something which they must conquer in the first hours after awaking. I am sure that many of you are familiar with this feeling in the morning, where one knows that one has not slept quite in the ordinary way; but that something was there which has left a certain sense of difficulty, that will take some time to overcome when one regains consciousness in the morning. This is an indication of that *third condition of sleep*, the content of which can be apprehended only through Intuition. It is a condition which is of great significance to the human being.

"When they are in the lightest sleep human beings are still actually concerned with a great deal that belongs to the experiences of waking consciousness. In a certain sense they still participate in their breathing processes; they also participate, although not from within but from without, in the blood circulation and the other processes of the body. In the *second condition of sleep*, they do not actually participate in the processes of their bodily life; they are concerned with a world that is common both to the body and to the soul. Some element connected with the body plays over into the soul, just as something passes over from the light into the plant when it is developing in the light of day. But when they are in the *third condition of sleep*, there is something within them which—if I may so express it—has become mineral; for in this state the salts of the body are especially strongly deposited. During this *third state of sleep* a very strong storing up of salts takes place in the physical body—with their souls, human beings live in the inner being of the mineral world.

"Now let us imagine that the following experiment may be made. You lie down in bed and fall into a light sleep from which dreams may emerge into ordinary consciousness. You pass over into a deeper sleep from which no dreams proceed; but in which the soul is still connected with the physical body. You then enter into a sleep in which strong accumulations of salts take place in the physical body. The soul can have no relation to what is thus taking place in the body. However, if you had placed beside your bed a mountain crystal, it would be possible for you to enter with your soul right into the inner being of the crystal; you would perceive it from within outwards. This is not possible either in the *first or in the second condition of sleep.* In the *first state of sleep*, the content of which can enter into the dream, you would, had you dreamed of the crystal, still perceive it as some kind of crystal—it would certainly be a shadowy experience, but something of the nature of a crystal would be there. In the second state of sleep the crystal would be experienced in a less definite sense; and if you could then still dream—that is not possible in the ordinary way, but we will imagine it to be so—then you would have the experience that the crystal becomes indefinite and forms itself into a kind of sphere or ellipsoid, and then recedes again. But if you could dream in the deepest sleep; that is, if you could bring into it the consciousness of Intuition—then out of this deepest sleep, this *third condition of sleep*, you would so experience the crystal that it would seem as though inwardly you followed these lines of form to the apex, and back again. You would experience the inner being of the crystal; you would be living within it. And so also in the case of other minerals. Not only would you experience the form, but also the inner forces. In short, the *third condition of sleep* is one which lifts human beings wholly out of their bodies and places them within the spiritual world. In this third stage of sleep, we live with the essential being of the spiritual world itself. That is, we stand within the essence, within the being, of Angels, Archangels and of all those beings whom we otherwise perceive outwardly, in their manifestations. Between waking and sleeping we see with our sense consciousness, as it were, the external manifestations of the Gods in nature. During sleep we enter either the world of pictures, in the first condition, or into the world of manifestation, the revelation of spiritual beings, in the second condition. And when we reach the third condition, we live within the divine spiritual beings themselves.

"Thus, just as in our waking consciousness we live the life of thinking, feeling and willing, so during sleep we either flow with the cosmic thoughts, or out of these cosmic thoughts the deeds of divine spiritual beings are revealed; or these spiritual beings so take us up into themselves that we rest within them with our souls. Just as thoughts and ideas are for the waking consciousness the clearest and most definite things of all, while feeling is darker and really a kind of dreaming, and willing the condition of the greatest insensibility—as it were a kind of sleep—so we have these three degrees of the sleeping consciousness. We have [*the first state of sleep*] the sleep in which ordinary consciousness experiences the dream and a higher clairvoyant consciousness – the cosmic thoughts. We have the *second state of sleep* which for the ordinary consciousness remains hidden; but so appears to the consciousness of Inspiration that everywhere the deeds of divine, spiritual beings are revealed. And we have the *third state of sleep*, which to Intuitional consciousness is life within the divine, spiritual beings themselves. This can be expressed by saying that we dive down, for instance, into the inner being of the minerals. This *third state of sleep* has, however, yet another element of great significance for the human being.

"In the *second stage of sleep*, as I have said, we find in the surging pictures, alternately appearing and disappearing, the cosmic being of the Angels, Archangels, and so on. But we find ourselves as well. We find ourselves as beings of soul; not, however, as we now are, but as we were before birth, before conception. We learn to know how we have lived between death and a new birth. This belongs to this second world [of sleep]. And every time we pass through dreamless sleep, we live in this same world in which we lived before we descended into our physical body. But when we pass over into the *third condition of sleep* and are able to awake there, when the consciousness of Intuition awakes, then we experience our destiny—our karma. We know then why in this life certain capacities are ours as results of a previous life. We know why in this life we have been led into connection with this or that personality; we learn to know our destiny, our karma.

"Before the Mystery of Golgotha, in the period of evolution before the appearance of Christ on Earth, human beings—we ourselves in earlier incarnations—entered very often into this third condition of sleep. But before they sank down into this sleep their Angels appeared and raised them out of it again. This is the significant thing: we can always raise ourselves out of the *first state of sleep*, and out of the *second state of sleep*, but not out of *the third state of sleep*. Before the appearance of Christ on Earth we must have died in this *third state of sleep* if Angels, or some other beings, had not raised us out of it. Since the appearance of Christ, the Christ-force has been united with the Earth. Every time that we must awaken out of this *third state of sleep*, the Christ-force which came to be united with the Earth through the Mystery of Golgotha must come to our aid. The human being can enter into the inner being of the crystal but cannot emerge again without the Christ-force."

The Forming of Destiny in Sleeping and Waking, Lecture I, Berne, April 6, 1923, GA 224

"One quality alone brings the Ego, during sleep, into right connection with the Archai, namely true human love, universal and unselfish love for human beings, sincere interest in every fellow man with whom life brings us into contact. I do not mean sympathy or antipathy, which are merely the outcome of something we are not willing to overcome. True and genuine love for human beings during the waking state leads us, during sleep, to the bosom of the Archai. And there, while the Ego is resting in the bosom of these Beings, karma or destiny is shaped. A verdict is passed: 'I am satisfied with what I have performed with my arms and legs.' And out of the satisfaction or dissatisfaction is born a power that not only plays a part in the period immediately following death but continues on to the next Earthly life— the power to shape destiny aright, so that true balance and adjustment are brought about in all those things which in one Earthly life we have experienced in the Ego during sleep, in communion with the Archai.

"When the human being sleeps, he is not merely resting from the fatigues of his daily life. Here in the physical world, man sleeps, works and speaks with his physical body; but he is active too in the spiritual world, while he is asleep. Since materialism denies that ego and astral body exist and operate in full reality of being during sleep, materialism cannot possibly understand the world in its entirety. What is the 'moral world' to materialism? To materialism the 'moral world' is something the human being formulates in thought—something that has nothing to do with the actively creative powers of the world. But those who have true and penetrating perception of human life know that man lives within the moral world-order during sleep just as truly as during waking life he lives in air and light. This again leads us to something more that it is essential we should understand.

"The workings of speech (and the same holds good for karma, too) accompany us when we die. Through the course of our life, we have been connected—rightly, or perhaps inadequately—with the world of the Archangels. This relationship has repeated itself in every period of sleep, and we bear with us through the Gate of Death into the spiritual world what has been given us by the Archangels during sleep. We can then find the way rightly into the spiritual world which is, indeed, the Logos, the world consisting of cosmic principles which have their images in the words of speech; we can find our way into the spiritual world to live out there our life between death and a new birth.

"But the matter is not so simple. After death we have no physical body; we are able to turn to good account what the Archangels have conferred upon us from our periods of sleep. But when as physical human beings on the Earth, we wake from sleep, we have again to descend into a physical body. The Archai cannot bestow upon us the power to do this. Still higher spiritual hierarchies must add their work, namely, the Beings designated in *Occult Science* the Exusiai and the Kyriotetes. Into the urges, instincts and desires of the physical body—which offer resistance to us—these Higher Beings must introduce the fruits of what we have achieved in communion with the Archangels through the spirituality of speech; and this now flames up within us, as the voice of conscience. When that which we bring out of sleep into the body lights up as the voice of conscience, there is working, in this voice, all that has been bestowed by the Hierarchy of the Exusiai and Kyriotetes—a Hierarchy more sublime than that of the Archangels.

"In thought we can be free. But in order to use this freedom aright in the physical body, the proper equilibrium must be established in waking and sleeping life because we must be united not only with the Archai but also with the Dynamis.

"The highest spiritual hierarchies of all—Seraphim, Cherubim and Thrones—bear our deeds out into the universe. From out of sleep, Exusiai, Dynamis, Kyriotetes bear as moral power into our bodily nature what we grasp in thoughts: Seraphim, Cherubim, and Thrones bear this out into the universe, so that our own moral forces become world-creative forces.

"Sleep comes over man for this very purpose—that he may, himself, draw out of the spiritual world the power he needs for his physical life.

"And now, from this point of view, study the connection of what I have sketched today in outline with my *Philosophy of Spiritual Activity*. As I have stated with emphasis there, it is not a matter of establishing the theory that the will must be free; but that the thought must be free. *The thought must control the will if man is to be a free being*. But a man's life must be suitably directed and ordered if the will is not to present insuperable hindrance to the thought that is free. As men in the physical world, we can make our thought free. Feeling becomes free only when we have established a true relationship with the Archangels; will becomes free when we have established a true relationship with the Archai.

"The living content of speech, as well as all that lives in our limbs, passes out, during sleep, together with the soul and spirit. Astral body and Ego go forth; but the ether-body remains with the physical body. The thinking that is bound up with the ether body continues within the ether-body; but we know nothing in ordinary consciousness of how this ether-body thinks from the time of falling asleep to that of waking, because we are outside it. It is not true that thinking ceases during sleep; we think from the moment of falling asleep until we wake. Man's thoughts are in perpetual flow in his ether-body, only he is unaware of it. Not until the moment when he returns to the body do the thoughts light up in his consciousness. Man can become free in his life of thought because his thoughts are bound, through the ether-body, with the physical life of Earth; for he has been placed upon the Earth in order that he may become free. From the spiritual world alone can he draw the power of freedom—the power that leads to freedom in feeling and in will.

"We can thus understand that there is a true relationship between freedom and karma; for freedom is connected with those members of man's being (physical body and ether-body) which remain behind during sleep. Karma is woven by the Ego during the period of sleep; that is to say, in a realm beyond and apart from those members wherein freedom has its foundations. Karma does not weave the texture of free or unfree thoughts; karma weaves feeling and will. Karma emerges from the depths of human nature, out of the 'dreaming' feeling and the 'sleeping' will."

Education, Section VII—*The Rhythmic System, Sleeping and Waking, Initiation,* Ilkley, August 11, 1923, GA 307

"In our modern civilization, where all eyes are concentrated on outer, material things, no attention is given to the consideration of the state of sleep; although man devotes to it one-third of his earthly life. This alternating rhythm of our waking and sleeping is of the greatest possible significance. Never should it be thought that man is inactive while he sleeps. He is inactive only insofar as the outer, external world is concerned; but as regards the health of his body, and more especially the welfare of his soul and spirit; sleep is all-important. True education can provide for a right life of sleep, for the activities which belong to man's waking hours are carried over into the condition of sleep, and this is especially the case with the child.

"Now because we generate this process of inner combustion, we bring about something in our organism that sleep alone can rectify. In a certain sense we should literally burn up our bodies if sleep did not perpetually reduce combustion to its right degree of intensity. All this must again be understood in a subtle sense and not in the crude sense of Natural Science. Sleep regulates the inner burning by spreading it over the whole organism; whereas otherwise, it would confine itself to the organs of movement."

The Evolution of Consciousness, The Relation of Man to the Three Worlds, August 23, 1923, Pennaenmawr, GA 227

"Dreams, of which I have already said something, pointing out that they should not be given too much importance in ordinary life on Earth, are nevertheless of immeasurable significance to those wishing to gain knowledge of man's relation to the super-sensible world. They do indeed lead to that realm of experience where a man comes in contact with the super-sensible world, and the laws of nature cease to hold good. Thus, the world of dream-pictures is really like a veil concealing the spiritual world, and we can say: Here we have a man, and there a dream-veil behind which lies the spiritual world. It makes a great difference, however, whether we enter the spiritual world unconsciously, as we do in dreams, or consciously through Imagination and Inspiration. For if we enter it consciously, everything there appears different from the physical world of nature. Behind the veil of the dream, behind what the Greeks called "chaos", the moral world is found to be just as real as is the world of nature here in the sense-world, where the laws of nature rule. But the chaotic quality of the dream, its whirling confusion, shows that its connection with the world lying behind the veil of chaos is a very special one.

"It is really possible to speak of this world only when one's studies have reached the point to which these lectures have brought us. All that in his ordinary state of consciousness a man sees of the external world is merely its outward manifestation; in reality this is a great illusion. For behind it all is that spiritual reality which is active in it. When a man dreams, he actually sinks down into this spiritual reality, though without being properly prepared, so that what he meets appears to him in this whirling confusion. Thus, to begin with, our chief task is to learn why in dreams a man enters a world which, compared with that of nature, is so disorganized, so chaotic.

"Three or four thousand years ago, as men were entering sleep, there arose in their souls like a dream a picture of the Guardian. They passed him by. And as they were returning from sleep to ordinary life, once again this picture appeared. The warnings they received on entering and leaving the spiritual world were not so clear as the warnings which I have said are given to those entering the spiritual world through Inspiration and Imagination. But as they fell asleep, and again as they awoke, they had a dreamlike experience of passing the Guardian of the Threshold, not unlike their other instinctive perceptions of the spiritual world. Further progress in the evolution of humanity—as we shall see in later lectures—required that man should gain his freedom by losing his spiritual vision, and he had to forfeit that half-sleeping, half-waking state during which he was able to behold, at least in a kind of dream, the majestic figure of the Guardian of the Threshold.

"Nowadays, between going to sleep and waking, a man passes the Guardian but does not know it. He is blind and deaf to the

Guardian, and that is why he finds himself in a dream world which is so completely disorganized.

"Now consider quite impartially the different way in which the people of older epochs knew how to speak of their dreams. Because of ignoring the Guardian every morning, every evening, and twice every time he takes an afternoon nap, a man today experiences this utter disorder and chaos in his dream-world. This can be seen in the form taken by any dream.

"Only think, when we cross the Threshold—and we do so each time we go to sleep—there stands the majestic Guardian. He cannot be ignored without everything we meet in the spiritual world becoming disordered. How this happens is best seen in the metamorphosis undergone by the orderly thinking proper to the physical, naturalistic world when this passes into the imagery of dreams. Individual dreams can show this very clearly.

"When, ignoring the Guardian, we cross the Threshold, we confront three worlds, and we can make nothing of them because we partly carry over into the world of spirit the outlook we are familiar with in the waking world. The spiritual world, however, asserts its own order to a certain extent. Then the following may come about. Imagine you are asleep in bed. At first with your feeling, with the middle part of your being, you are entirely under the influence of sleep. Then the blanket slips; part of your body gets chilled, and it enters your dream consciousness that some part of you is unclothed. Now, because you are all at sea in the spiritual world and do not connect the sensation with any particular part of yourself, this feeling spreads and you fancy you are without any clothes at all. It may be only a bit of your body that is exposed; but that bit becoming cold makes you feel bare all over.

"Now in your dream you are still concerned with an impulse of will holding good when you are awake—which is to put on clothes when bare. In your sleep, however, you feel: I cannot put them on, something is preventing me. You are unable to move your limbs and you become conscious of this in your dream.

"You see how it is? These two things, I feel I've nothing on, and I cannot put on my clothes—the physical world being no longer there to combine the two, one of which belongs to world 2, the other to world 1—are wrongly combined in your dream. And because in that same night you had thought about going for a walk, this also enters the course of the dream. Three separate conditions arise: I am going for a walk; I am horrified to find I have nothing on; I cannot put my clothes on.

"Now just think. These three things, which in our ordinary materialistic life can be logically combined, fall asunder when, in passing by you ignore the Guardian of the Threshold.

"In this situation you feel yourself in three parts, among strangers, exposed to view on all sides without clothes and without power to put them on. That is your dream experience. What is connected for you in ordinary life through natural logic is separated in your dream and connected, chaotically, in conformity with the custom you take with you across the Threshold. You connect it as if in the spiritual world, too, one must concern oneself with garments. Because of ignoring the Guardian of the Threshold, you carry over into the spiritual world a custom suited to the physical world. You connect the three worlds chaotically, according to the laws of the physical world, and you feel yourself to be in this situation.

"In countless dreams the essential thing is that when we pass the Threshold without heeding the Guardian's warning, what we perceive here in the physical, naturalistic world as a harmonious unity falls apart, and we are confronted by three different worlds. By faithfully observing the warning given by the

Guardian of the Threshold, we must find the way to unite these three worlds. Today, a man in his dreams finds himself faced by these three worlds—it was not so to the same extent for anyone in older epochs, as can be seen from the dreams recorded in the Old Testament—and he then tries to connect the three worlds in accordance with laws valid in physical life. That is the reason for the chaotic connections in the three worlds, as they are experienced by a man of today.

"You will see, therefore, that dreams can show us this serious fact—that when we cross the Threshold to the spiritual world we are at once faced with three worlds, and that we have both to enter them and to leave them in the right way. Dreams can teach us a very great deal about the physical world of the senses, as it is today, and also about that other world—the world of soul and spirit."

Knowledge of Higher Worlds and its Attainment, Section VII, *The Continuity of Consciousness*, GA 10

"Human life runs its course in three alternating states or conditions: namely, waking, dreaming sleep, and dreamless sleep. The attainment of the higher knowledge of spiritual worlds can be readily understood if a conception is formed of the changes occurring in these three conditions, as experienced by one seeking such higher knowledge. When no training has been undertaken to attain this knowledge, human consciousness is continually interrupted by the restful interval of sleep. During these intervals the soul knows nothing of the outer world, and equally little of itself. Only at certain periods do dreams emerge from the deep ocean of insensibility, dreams linked to the occurrences of the outer world or the conditions of the physical body. At first, dreams are only regarded as a particular manifestation of sleep-life, and thus only two states are generally spoken of, namely, sleeping and waking. For spiritual science, however, dreams have an independent significance apart from the other two conditions.

"In the previous chapter a description was given of the alteration ensuing in the dream-life of the person undertaking the ascent to higher knowledge. His dreams lose their meaningless, irregular, and disconnected character and form themselves more and more into a world of law and order. With continued development, not only does this new world born out of the dream-world come to be in no way inferior to outer physical reality as regards its inner-truth, but facts reveal themselves in it representing a higher reality in the fullest sense of the word. Secrets and riddles lie concealed everywhere in the physical world. In the latter, the effects are seen of certain higher facts; but no one can penetrate to the causes when perception is merely confined to his senses. These causes are partly revealed to the student in the condition described above and developed out of dream-life, a condition, however, which by no means remains stationary. True, he must not regard these revelations as actual knowledge so long as the same things do not also reveal themselves during ordinary waking-life. But in time he achieves this as well: he develops this faculty of carrying over into waking consciousness the condition he created for himself out of dream-life. Thus, something new is introduced into the world of his senses that enriches it. Just as a person born blind that is successfully operated on will recognize the surrounding objects as enriched by all that the eye perceives; likewise, will anyone having become clairvoyant in the above manner perceive the whole world surrounding him peopled with new qualities, things, beings, and so forth. He now need no longer wait for his dreams to live in another world; but he can at any suitable moment put himself into the above condition for the purpose of higher perception. This condition then acquires a significance for him similar to the perception, in ordinary life, of things with active senses as opposed to inactive senses. It can truly be said that the student opens the eyes of his soul and beholds things which necessarily remain concealed from the bodily senses.

"Now this condition is only transitional to still higher stages of knowledge. If the pupil continues his esoteric exercises he will find in due time, that the radical change described above, does not confine itself to his dream-life, but that this transformation also extends to what was previously a condition of deep-dreamless-sleep. Isolated conscious experiences begin to interrupt the complete insensibility of this deep-sleep. Perceptions previously unknown to him emerge from the pervading unknown to him emerge from the pervading darkness of sleep. It is, of course, not easy to describe these perceptions; for our language is only adapted to the physical world, and therefore only approximate terms can be found to express what does not at all belong to that world.

"Some idea can be given of those experiences which emerge from the unconsciousness of deep-sleep if they are compared to a kind of *hearing*. We may speak of *audible* tones and words. While the experiences during dream-sleep may correctly be designated as a kind of seeing, the facts observed during deep-sleep may be compared to auditory sound impressions. (It should be remarked in passing that for the spiritual world, too, the faculty of *seeing* or *beholding* remains the higher faculty. There, too, colors are higher than sounds and words. The student's first perceptions in this world do not yet extend to the higher colors; but only to the lower tones. Only because man, according to his general development, is already more qualified for the world revealing itself in dream-sleep does he at once perceive colors there. He is less qualified for the higher world unveiling itself in deep-sleep; therefore, the first revelations of it he receives are in tones and words; later on he can rise also to the level of colors and forms.)"

Initiation and its Results, Section III, *Dream Life*, GA 10

"An intimation that the pupil has arrived at the stage of evolution described in the foregoing chapter is the change which comes over his dream-life. Until now his dreams were confused and haphazard; but now they begin to assume a more regular character. Their pictures begin to arrange themselves in an orderly way, like the phenomena of daily life. He can discern in them laws, causes, and effects. The contents of his dreams will likewise change. Until now he discerned only the reverberations of daily life, mixed impressions of his surroundings or of his physical condition; but now, before him pictures of a world appear with which he had no acquaintance. At first, indeed, the general nature of his dreams will remain as of old, insofar as the dream differentiates itself from waking phenomena by presenting in symbolic form whatever it wishes to express. This dramatization cannot have escaped the notice of any attentive observer of dream-life. For instance, you may dream that you are catching some horrible creature and experiencing an unpleasant sensation in your hand. You wake up to discover that you are tightly holding a piece of the blanket. The perception does not express itself plainly; but only through the allegorical image. Or you may dream that you are flying from some pursuer; and in consequence you experience fear. On waking up you find that during sleep you have been suffering from heart palpitations. Furthermore, a stomach that is full of indigestible food can cause uneasy dream-pictures. Occurrences in the neighborhood of the sleeping person may also reflect themselves allegorically in dreams. The striking of a clock may evoke the picture of soldiers marching-by to the sound of their drums. Or a falling chair can become the origin of a complete dream-drama in which the sound of falling is translated into a gun report, and so forth. The more regulated dreams of the person whose etheric body has begun its development have also this allegorical method of expression; but they will cease to repeat merely the facts of the physical environment or of the sense-body. As these dreams which owe their origin to such things become orderly, they are mixed up with similar dream-pictures which are the expression of things and events from another world. Here one has experiences that lie beyond the range of one's waking consciousness. Now it must never be thought that any genuine mystic will then make the things which in this manner he experiences in dreams the basis of any authoritative account of the higher world. One must only consider such dream-experiences as hints of a higher development. Very soon, as a further result of this, we find that the pictures of the dreaming student are no longer, as hitherto, withdrawn by the guidance of a careful intellect; but are regulated thereby, and methodically considered like the conceptions and impressions of the waking consciousness. The difference between this dream-consciousness and the waking state grows ever smaller and smaller. The dreamer becomes, in the fullest meaning of the word, awake in his dream-life: that is to say, he can feel himself to be the master and leader of the pictures which then appear.

"During his dreams the individual actually finds himself in a world which is other than that of his physical senses. But if he possesses only un-evolved spiritual organs, he can receive from that world only the confused dramatizations already mentioned. It would only be as much at his disposal as would be the sense-world to a being equipped with nothing but the most rudimentary of eyes. In consequence, in this world, he could only discern the reflections and reverberations of ordinary life. Yet in dreams he can see these, because his soul interweaves its daily perceptions as pictures into the stuff of which that other world consists. It must here be clearly understood that in addition to the work-a-day conscious life, one leads in this world a second and unconscious existence. Everything that one perceives or thinks becomes impressed upon this other world. Only if the lotus-flowers are evolved can one perceive these impressions. Now certain minute beginnings of the lotus-flowers are always at the disposal of anyone. During daily consciousness he cannot perceive with them because the impressions made on him are very faint. It is for similar reasons that during the daytime one cannot see the stars. For they cannot strike our perceptions when opposed by the fierce and active sunlight, and it is just in this way that faint spiritual impressions cannot make themselves felt in opposition to the masterful impressions of the physical senses. When the door of outward sense is closed in sleep, these impressions can emerge confusedly, and then the dreamer remembers what he has experienced in another world. Yet, as already remarked, at first these experiences are nothing more than that which conceptions related to the physical senses have impressed on the spiritual world. Only the developed lotus-flowers [chakras] make it possible for manifestations which are unconnected with the physical world to show themselves. Out of the development of the etheric body arises a full knowledge concerning the impressions that are conveyed from one world to another. With this the pupil's communication with a new world has begun.

He must now—by means of the instructions given in his occult training—first of all acquire a twofold nature. It must become possible for him during waking hours to recall quite consciously the beings he has observed in dreams. If he has acquired this faculty, he will then become able to make these observations during his ordinary waking-state. For his attention will have become so concentrated upon spiritual impressions that these impressions need no longer vanish in the light of those which come through the senses; but are, as it were, always at hand."

Manifestations of the Unconscious Dreams, Hallucinations, Visons, Somnanbulism, Mediumship, Berlin, March 21, 1918, GA 67

"Everyone is familiar with the external characteristics of the upsurging and ebbing life of pictures arising in dreams. I shall speak of a few of these characteristics only. The dream arises as the result of some definite instigation. Firstly, there are dreams which have been instigated by the senses. A dream may arise because a clock is ticking away beside us. In certain circumstances the pendulum-beats become the trampling of horses, or perhaps something else. Certain sense-images, therefore, are found in the dream. I lay particular stress on this, for dream-experience bases itself upon numerous impressions received by the outer senses. But what works upon the outer senses never works in the dream in the same form as in the ordinary waking life of day. The sense-impression is always transformed into symbolism—a transformation that is actually brought about by the soul-life.

"But dreams can also be due to inner stimuli, and again it is not the stimuli as such which appear, instead it is the sense-image that has been transformed, cast into symbolism, by the soul. For example, someone dreams of a very hot stove; as a result, he wakes up with his heart thumping. Dreams of flying, which occur very frequently, are due, as a rule, to some kind of abnormal process taking place in the lungs during sleep. Hundreds of such examples could be quoted and the different categories of dreams enumerated at great length. Although we cannot enter exhaustively into the deeper aspects of sleep, I want still to speak of certain points.

"Literature offers no evidence of particular success in discovering the elements in the human soul capable of showing what is actually going on in the soul when bringing about the transformations of the outer stimuli into dreams. Here it must be said that what is actually working in the dream is not the faculty which in ordinary waking life enables man to link one mental picture to another. What is of paramount importance in man's life of feeling is always the decisive factor in the structure assumed by the pictures of dream. From this point-of-view therefore, the dream takes shape in order that certain tensions in the soul may be overcome. The picture which, as such, has no special significance, is born from this need to lead tension over to relaxation, relaxation over to tension. The soul conjures before itself something that can be an imaginative indication of the real gist of the matter.

"Examination of the whole range of the life of dream brings to light two peculiar features which must be particularly borne in mind. The one is that what is usually called logic plays no part in dreams. For the dream has a rule entirely different from that of ordinary logic by the way in which it passes from one object to the other. Naturally you will be able to insist that many dreams take a perfectly logical course. But this is only apparently the case, as everyone who can observe these things intimately knows. If dream-pictures present themselves in logical sequence, the reason is not that you produce this sequence during the dream; but rather, that you are placing side-by-side, mental images which you have already connected together logically at some time, or which have been so connected by some agency in life. In such a case, logic in the dream is reminiscence; the logic has been imported into the dream; for the action of the dream does not in itself proceed according to the rules of ordinary logic.

"Moral judgment is also silent in dreams. It is well known that in a dream a man may commit all kinds of misdeeds of which he would be ashamed in waking life. It can be argued that conscience begins to stir in dreams, that it often makes itself felt in a very remarkable way. Think only of the dreams contained in Shakespeare's plays—poets generally have a good reason for such things—and you will find that they might appear to suggest that moral reproaches make themselves particularly conspicuous through dreams. What is true is that in the dream we are snatched away from the faculty of ordinary moral judgment which in connection with human beings in outer life we must and can exercise. If the dream seems to present moral ideas and moral reproaches in concrete pictures, this is not due to the fact that as dreamers we form moral judgments; but that when we act morally the soul feels a certain inner satisfaction; we are inwardly gratified about something to which we can give moral assent. It is this state of satisfaction, not moral judgment, that presents itself to the soul in the dream. Neither logic or moral judgment play any part at all in dreams.

"Pictures do indeed surge up and fade away in dreams but their actual relation to the external world is not changed; the form assumed by the pictures is such that this relation remains as it was. The relationship to the external world, to that environment which gives contour to the outer sense impressions, and approaches man as he opens his senses during waking life—*this does not penetrate into the dream*. Impressions can indeed be made upon a man; but the characteristics of what the senses make out of those impressions are absent. The soul puts an emblem, a symbol, in the place of the ordinary, plain impression. Therefore, the actual relation to the outer world does not change. In the normal dream the human being is as shut off from the external world as he is in normal sleep; he is also shut off from his own body. What rises-up from his bodily nature does not come to direct expression as is the case when he is united in the normal way with his body.

"Attempts to explain the nature of dreams simply by using methods and sources available to external science will always be in vain, because there is nothing with which the dream can truly be compared. It occurs in the ordinary world as a kind of miraculous happening. That is the essential point. The spiritual investigator alone is in the position of being able to compare the dream with something else.

"The first stage of knowledge of the spiritual world is then capable of being compared with the unconscious activity at work in dreams. A man who makes real progress in knowledge of the spiritual world gradually begins to experience that his dreams themselves are changing. They become more and more rational, and crazy images gradually turn into pictures which have real meaning; the whole life of dream becomes charged with meaning. In this way the spiritual investigator comes to know the peculiar nature of the relation between the life of dream and the kind of life he must adopt in the interests of spiritual investigation. This puts him in the position of being able to say what it is in the soul that is actually doing the dreaming. For he comes to know something besides, namely, the condition of soul in which he finds himself while experiencing the pictures and ideas of genuine Imagination. He knows that with his soul he is then within the spiritual world. When this particular condition of the life of soul is experienced, it can be compared with the condition of the soul in dreams. This scrupulous comparison reveals that what is actually dreaming in the soul; for what is active in the soul while the chaotic actions of dreams are in play—*is the spiritual, eternal core of man's being.* When he dreams, man is in the world to which he belongs as a being of spirit-and-soul. There you have the facts of the matter. The dream therefore points to deep subconscious and unconscious grounds of the life of soul. But the pictures unfolded by the dream are only a veiling of what is actually being experienced in the course of it.

"A man who is really free from his body in spiritual experience has the spiritual world before him with its happenings and its beings; on the other hand, the dreamer has not yet awakened his consciousness to the degree where this is possible for him. For his soul resorts to the reminiscences of ordinary life and the dream arises when the soul impacts the body. The dream is not experienced in the body; but it is caused by the impact of the soul on the body. Hence the things which constitute the course of his life present themselves to the dreamer; but grouped in such a way that they bring to expression the inner tendencies of which I have spoken. Therefore, in reality the dream is experienced by a man's own essential being of soul and spirit. But it is not the eternal that is experienced; what is experienced is the temporal. It is the eternal that is consciously active in the dream; but this activity is mediated by the transitory, the transient. The essential point is that in the dream the eternal is experiencing the temporal, the transitory—*the content of life.*

"I have now briefly explained the nature of dream as viewed in the light of spiritual science and why it is that the content of the dream is not an expression of what is actually going on in the soul when relaxation follows tension and tension follows relaxation. In the life of dream the soul is in the world of the Eternal, free from the body. But what enters into the consciousness as the clothing of this experience arises from the connection with the ordinary circumstances of life.

"In point-of-fact, the dream passes only slightly into the abnormal life of soul. Spiritual Science shows that the soul is free from the body in dreams, that the experiences of dreams are independent of bodily experiences; they are separated from the link with the outer world that is present in waking life. In the dream, man is actually free from his body.

"Among all these manifestations the life of dream alone remains within the sphere of the normal, because in dream the human being is not experiencing through the bodily constitution but through the spirit and soul; as a being of spirit and soul he strikes up against the body and the physical experiences. Hence in respect of the life of dream too, man is able to exercise correctives and to give it its rightful place within the rest of life. In dream, man experiences the spiritual world in such a way that as the result of impact with the bodily constitution, sense-images take shape.

"When it is realized that through the seemingly chaotic life of dream man is admonished to find the path into the true spiritual world, the significance of such study becomes evident. A great world-riddle is knocking here at the door of human life. This world-riddle is the dream with its strange pictures in which logic and moral judgment are lacking; but which are a definite signpost to the spiritual world itself. The realm of dream is an admonition to man to seek for the spiritual world, and the aim of Spiritual Science is to fulfill this admonition."

Knowledge of the Higher Worlds and its Attainment, Lecture VI, *The Transformation of Dream Life,* GA 10

"An intimation that the pupil has reached or will soon reach the stage of development described in the preceding chapter will be found in the change which comes over his dream-life. His dreams, hitherto confused and haphazard, now begin to assume a more regular character. Their pictures begin to succeed each other in sensible connection, like the thoughts and ideas of daily life. He can discern in them law, cause, and effect. The content, too, of his dreams is changed. While hitherto he discerned only reminiscences of daily life and transformed impressions of his surroundings or of his physical condition, there now appear before him pictures of a world he has hitherto not known. At first the general character of his dream-life remains unchanged, insofar as dreams are distinguished from waking mental activity by the symbolic presentation of what they wish to express. No attentive observer of dream-life can fail to detect this characteristic. For instance, a person may dream that he has caught some horrible creature, and he feels an unpleasant sensation in his hand. He wakes to discover that he is tightly grasping a corner of the blanket. The truth is not presented to the mind, except through the medium of a symbolic image. A man may dream that he is flying from some pursuer and is stricken with fear. On waking, he finds that he has been suffering, during sleep, from palpitations of the heart. Disquieting dreams can also be traced to indigestible food. Occurrences in the immediate vicinity may also reflect themselves symbolically in dreams. The striking of a clock may evoke the picture of a troop of soldiers marching-by to the beat of a drum. A falling chair may be the occasion of a whole dream drama in which the sound of the fall is reproduced as the report of a gun, and so forth. The more regulated dreams of esoteric students whose etheric body has begun its development retain this symbolic method of expression; but they will cease merely to reflect the reality connected with the physical body and physical environment. As the dreams due to the latter causes become more connected, they are mingled with similar pictures expressing things and events of another world. These are the first experiences lying beyond the range of waking consciousness.

"Yet no true mystic will ever make his experiences in dreams the basis of any authoritative account of the higher world. Such dreams must be merely be considered as providing the first hint of a higher development. Very soon and as a further result, the student's dreams will no longer remain beyond the reach of intellectual guidance as heretofore; but on the contrary, they will be mentally controlled and supervised like the impressions and conceptions of waking consciousness. Gradually the difference between dream and waking consciousness grows ever smaller. The dreamer remains awake in the fullest sense of the word during his dream-life; that is, he is aware of his mastery and control over his own vivid mental activity.

"During our dreams, we are actually in a world other than that of our senses; but with undeveloped spiritual organs we can form none other than the confused conceptions of it described above."

The Evolution of Consciousness, Lecture IV, *Dream Life*, Penmaenmawr, August 22, 1923, GA 227

"Between a man's waking life and his life in sleep—which yesterday I was able to picture for you at least in outline—there comes his dream-life. It may have little significance for the immediate actualities of daily existence; but it has the greatest imaginable significance for a deeper knowledge of both world and man. This is not only because what a dream signifies must, in the Spiritual Science spoken of here, be fully recognized, so that the study of it may lead on to many other matters; but also because of the particular importance of dream-life as a window, shall we say, through which certain other worlds, different from the one experienced by human beings when awake, shine into this ordinary world. So it is that the puzzling elements in dream pictures often call attention both to other worlds, below or above the one normally accessible, and also give some indication of the nature of these worlds.

"On the other hand, it is extraordinarily difficult from the standpoint of higher consciousness to go deeply into the enigmas of dream-life, for dreams have the power to lead people into the greatest imaginable illusions. It is precisely when dreams are in question that people are inclined to go wrong over the relation of something illusory to the reality behind it.

"Between falling asleep and waking we have our whole human life. We have to bring to bear on it all that as earthly beings we can conceive and think, and by this means try to unravel the strange forms taken by dreams. The great difficulty is to distinguish the immediate content of the dream, which may be sheer illusion, from the reality which lies behind it; for the reality may be something quite different. But anyone who gradually gets accustomed to finding his way among all the intricacies of dream-life will finally see that we need not pay much attention to the pictures conjured up before the soul; for these pictures are shaped by the etheric body left behind in bed. This etheric body is the bearer of our thoughts and conceptions, and these are absent from our real being during sleep. We have to separate the content of these conceptions from what I would call the dramatic course of the dream, and learn to fix our attention on the dramatic element so that it prompts questions such as: If I had this experience in waking life, would it give me immense pleasure? And, if I felt pleasure and had a sense of relief in this dream, was I heading in the dream for a catastrophe? Was I leaving some kind of exhibition and suddenly everything got into confusion and there was a crash and a disaster? Such questions must be given first place in the study of dreams—*not the thought-content but the dramatic incidents.*

"All this shows how we have to look for the key to a dream not—as is often done—by considering its content in an external way; but by studying its dramatic course and the effect it has on the dreamer's soul and spirit. Then, when our conceptual faculty has been strengthened by the exercises referred to in the past few days, we shall gradually progress from the illusory picture-world of the dream and be able to grasp through the dramatic element the true basis of all that we experience as super-sensible reality between going to sleep and waking.

"The dream takes events that could happen in the sense-world and makes them chaotic. Everything becomes different; everything is broken up. In effect, everything in daily life with definite connections loses them to a certain extent in dreams. If we want to picture what actually happens—or appears to happen—in a dream.

"The dream we have as we go to sleep and the dream we have just before waking both draw on the experiences of the day, break them up and give them all sorts of fantastic forms—at least we call them fantastic from the point-of-view of ordinary consciousness. The dissolving of a salt crystal in a liquid is a good simile for the kind of thing that happens inwardly in a dream.

"Dreams are a power which forcibly opposes nature's laws. While I am dreaming, the dream itself shows me that I am living in a world opposed to these laws, a world which refuses to be subject to them. While going to sleep in the evening and moving out of my physical and etheric bodies, I am still living half under the laws of nature, although I am already entering the world where they cease to be valid. Hence arises the confusion in the dream between natural laws and super-sensible laws; and it is the same while we are waking up again.

"Thus, we can say that each time we go to sleep we sink into a world where the laws of nature are not valid; and each time we wake we leave that world to re-enter a world subject to those laws. If we are to imagine the actual process, it is like this. Picture the dream-world as a sea in which you are living and assume that in the morning you wake out of the waves of dream-life—it is as if you arose out of the surge of those waves. You move from the realm of super-sensible law into the realm of intellectual, material law. And it seems to you as though everything you see in sharp outlines upon awakening was born out of the fluid and the volatile.

"When from the point-of-view of what is revealed to us on the path I have been describing here—the path leading through Imagination, Inspiration, Intuition, to higher knowledge and super-sensible worlds—when we follow all that goes on during our dreaming, sleeping and re-awaking, then we see that a man sleeps himself out of his daytime state into his life of sleep, out of which dreams may arise in a way that is chaotically vague, but also inwardly consistent. Behind, in bed, the physical body is left with the etheric body which is interwoven with the physical, giving it life, form, and the power of growth. This twofold entity is left in the bed.

"But another twofold entity goes out during sleep into a form of super-sensible existence which I might also describe to you in relation still to dream existence. For the higher knowledge given by Imagination, Inspiration, Intuition, presents itself in the following way.

"When a man goes out from his physical body and etheric body, his individuality resides in his astral body. Now, this astral body is made up of processes. Something happens in a man which develops out of his physical and etheric bodies, and it is these happenings which represent the astral body; whereas our concepts, our thoughts, are left behind in the etheric body.

"Within the astral body there is spiritualized light, and cosmic warmth permeated by the force of the capacity for love. All this is present in the astral body, and at the time of waking it dives down into the etheric body. There it is held up and appears as the weaving, the action, of the dream. It may also appear in this way when, freeing itself from the physical and etheric bodies, it leaves the world of concepts. Thus, it belongs to the nature of the astral body to carry us out from our physical and etheric bodies.

"Also during sleep the ego is active; but what it does is shown to us through dreams in illusory pictures. In earthly life we are unable to take in what is already being woven during sleep for our next life on Earth. At the beginning of this lecture, I explained how the dream, in the same confused way in which it presents the experiences of a past incarnation, also shows, in a chaotic form, what is prepared as a seed for humanity in future times.

"Hence the right interpretation of dreams leads us to recognize that they are like a window through which we have only to look in the right way—*a window into the super-sensible world.* Behind this window the ego is actively weaving, and this weaving goes on from one earthly life to the next. When we can interpret a dream rightly, then, through this window from the transitory world in which we live as earthly men, we already perceive that everlasting world, that eternity, to which in our true inner being we belong."

Anthroposophy, An Introduction, Section 8, Dreams, Imaginative Cognition and the Building of Destiny, Dornach, February 9, 1924, GA 234

"Yesterday I tried to show how a more intimate study of man's dream-life can lead us towards the Science of Initiation. To a certain extent, the point-of-view was that of ordinary consciousness. Today it will be my task to enter more deeply into the same subject-matter from the point-of-view of 'imaginative' cognition.

"For the moment we will neglect the difference between the two kinds of dreams discussed yesterday and consider dreams as such. It will be a sound approach to describe 'imaginative' vision in relation to dreams which a man endowed with [moral] imagination may have. Let us compare such a dream with the self-perception attained by the imaginative seer when he looks back upon his own being—when he observes imaginatively his own or another's organs—or, perhaps, the whole human being as a complete organism. You see, the appearance of the dream-world to imaginative consciousness is quite different from its appearance to ordinary consciousness. The same is true of the physical and etheric organisms. Now the imaginative seer can dream too; and under certain circumstances his dreams will be just as chaotic as those of other people. From his own experience he can quite well judge the world of dreams; for, side-by-side with the imaginative life that is inwardly coordinated, clear and luminous, the dream-world runs its ordinary course, just as it does side-by-side with waking life. I have often emphasized that one who attains really spiritual perception does not become a dreamer or enthusiast, living only in the higher worlds and not seeing external reality. People who are ever dreaming in higher worlds, or about them, and do not see external reality, are not Initiates; but rather, they should be considered from a pathological point-of-view, at least in the psychological sense of the term. The real knowledge of initiation does not estrange one from ordinary, physical life and its various relationships. On the contrary, it makes one a more painstaking, conscientious observer than without the faculty of seership. Indeed, we may say: If a man has no sense of ordinary realities, no interest in ordinary realities, no interest in the details of others' lives, if he is so 'superior' that he sails through life without troubling about its details—*he shows he is not a genuine seer*. A man with imaginative cognition—he may, of course, also have 'inspired' and 'intuitive' cognition (but at present I am only speaking of 'imagination')—is quite well acquainted with dreamlife from his own experience. Nevertheless, his conception of dreams is different. He feels the dream as something with which he is connected, with which he unites himself much more strongly than is possible through ordinary consciousness. He can take dreams more seriously. Indeed, only imagination justifies us taking our dreams seriously; for it enables us to look, as it were, behind dreaming and apprehend its dramatic course—its tensions, resolutions, catastrophes, and crises—rather than its detailed content. The individual content interests us less, even before we acquire imagination; we are more interested in studying whether the dream leads to a crisis, or to inner joy, to something that we find easy or that proves difficult, and the like.

"It is the course of the dream just that which does not interest ordinary consciousness and which I can only call the dramatic quality of the dream—that begins to interest us most. We see behind the scenes of dream-life and, in doing so, become aware that we have before us something related to man's spiritual being in quite a definite way. We see that, in a spiritual sense, the dream is the human being, as the seed is the plant. And in this 'seed-like' man we learn to grasp what is really foreign to his present life—just as the seed taken from the plant in the autumn of a given year is foreign to the plant's life of that year and will only be at home in the plant-growth of the following year. It is just this way of studying the dream that gives imaginative consciousness its strongest impressions; for, in our own dreaming being, we detect more and more that we bear within us something that passes over to our next life on Earth, germinating between death and a new birth and growing on into our next earthly life. It is the seed of this next earthly life that we learn to feel in the dream.

"The human head is withering most; and the dream appears to imaginative perception as an emanation of the human head. On the other hand, the metabolic and limb organism appears to imaginative vision to be withering least of all. It appears very similar to the ordinary dream; it is least faded and most closely united, in form and content, with the future of man. The rhythmic organization contained in the chest is the connecting link between them, holding the balance.

"On the other hand, when we try to understand the metabolic and limb system with imaginative consciousness, we say to ourselves: Your keen intellect does not help you here; you ought properly to sleep and dream of man; for man only apprehends this part of his organization by dreaming of it while awake.

"So, you see, we must proceed to a highly differentiated mode of perception when we begin to study man's physical organization imaginatively. We must become *clever, terribly clever*, when we study his head. On the other hand, we must become *dreamers* when studying his system of limbs and metabolism. And we must really swing to and fro, as it were, between dreaming and waking if we want to grasp, in imaginative vision, the wonderful structure of man's rhythmic system. But all this appears as the relic of his last life on Earth. What he experiences in the waking state is the relic of his last life; this plays into his present life, giving him as much as I ascribed to him yesterday when I said of his life of action, for example, that only as much of man's actions as he can dream of is really done by himself; the rest is done by the gods in and through him. The present is active to this extent; all the rest comes from his former earthly lives. We see that this is so when we have a man before us and perceive his withering physical organization. And if we look at what man knows of himself while he dreams—dreams in his sleep—we have before us what man is preparing for the next life on Earth. These things can be easily distinguished.

"Consider man's life on Earth. There are waking states interrupted again and again by sleep. Now a man who is not a 'sleepy head' will spend about a third of his life asleep. During this third he does, in fact, live through the spiritual counterpart of his deeds; only he knows nothing of it, his dreams merely casting-up ripples to the surface. Much of the spiritual counterpart is perceived in dreams; but only in the form of weak surface-ripples. Nevertheless, in dee- sleep we do experience unconsciously the whole spiritual aspect of our daily life. So, we might put it this way: In our conscious daily life we experience what others think and feel, how they are helped or hindered by us; in sleep we experience unconsciously what the gods think about the deeds and thoughts of our waking life, though we know nothing of this. It is for this reason that one who sees into the secrets of life seems to himself so burdened with debt, so maimed—as I have described. All this has remained in the subconscious. Now after death it is really lived through consciously. For this reason, man lives through the part of life he has slept through; i.e. about one-third, in time, of his earthly life. Thus, when he has passed through death, he lives through his nights again, backwards; only, what he lived through unconsciously, night-by-night, now becomes conscious."

Anthroposophy, An Introduction, Lecture VII, *Dream-Life and External Reality*, Dornach, February 8, 1924, GA 234

"Let us now consider this dream-life as it presents itself to us. We can distinguish two different kinds of dreams. The first conjures pictures of outer experiences before our soul. Years ago, or a few days maybe, we experienced this or that in a definite way; now a dream conjures up a picture more-or-less similar—usually dissimilar—to the external experience. If we discover the connection between this dream picture and the external experience, we are at once struck by the transformation the latter has undergone. We do not usually relate the dream-picture to a particular experience in the outer world; for the resemblance does not strike us. Nevertheless, if we look more closely at this type of dream-life that conjures outer experiences in transformed pictures before the soul, we find that something in us takes hold of these experiences; we cannot, however, retain them as we can in the waking-state, when we have full use of our bodily organs and experience the images of memory which resemble external life as far as possible. In memory we have pictures of outer life that are more-or-less true. Of course, there are people who dream in their memories; but this is regarded as abnormal. In our memories we have, more-or-less, true pictures, in our dreams, transformed pictures of outer life. That is one kind of dream.

There is, however, another kind, and this is really much more important for a knowledge of the dream-life. It is the kind in which, for example, a man dreams of seeing a row of white pillars, one of which is damaged or dirty; he wakes up with this dream and finds he has toothache. He then sees that the row of pillars 'symbolizes' the row of teeth; one tooth is aching, and this is represented by the damaged or, perhaps, dirty pillar. Or a man may wake up dreaming of a seething stove and find he has a heart palpitation. Or he is distressed in his dream by a frog approaching his hand; he takes hold of the frog. He shudders and wakes up to find he is holding a corner of his blanket, grasped in sleep. These things can go much further. A man may dream of all kinds of snake-like forms and wake up with intestinal pains.

"So, we see that there is a second kind of dream which gives pictorial, symbolic expression to man's inner organs. When we have grasped this, we learn to interpret many dream-figures in just this way. For example, we may dream of entering a vaulted cellar. The ceiling is black and covered with cobwebs; a repulsive sight. We wake up to find we have a headache. The interior of the skull is expressed in the vaulted cellar; we even notice that the cerebral convolutions are symbolized in the peculiar formations constituting the vault. If we pursue our studies further in this direction, we find that all our organs can appear in dreams in this pictorial way.

"Here, indeed, is something that points very clearly, by means of the dream, to the whole inner life of man. There are people who, while actually asleep and dreaming, compose subjects for quite good paintings. If you have studied these things, you will know what particular organ is depicted, though in an altered, symbolic form. Such paintings sometimes possess unusual beauty; and when the artist is told what organ he has really symbolized so beautifully, he is quite startle; for he hasn't the same respect for his organs that he has for his paintings!

"These two kinds of dreams can be easily distinguished by one who is prepared to study the world of dreams in an intimate way. In one kind of dream, we have pictures of experiences undergone in the outer world: in the other, pictorial representations of our own internal organs.

"Now it is comparatively easy to pursue the study of dreams as far as this. Most people whose attention has been called to the existence of these two kinds will recall experiences of their own that justify this classification.

"But to what does this classification point? Well, if you examine the first kind of dreams, studying the special kind of pictures contained, you find that widely different external experiences can be represented by the same dream; again, one and the same experience can be depicted in different people by different dreams.

"Now, if we start from here and examine dreams of this (first) type, we find that the pictures derive their whole character chiefly from the nature of the man himself, from the individuality of his ego. If we have an understanding of dreams—I say, of dreams, not of dream-interpretation—we can often learn to know a man better from his dreams than from observing his external life. When we study all that a person experiences in such dreams, we find that it always points back to the experience of the ego in the outer world.

"On the other hand, when we study the second kind of dream, we find that what it conjures before the soul in dream pictures is only experienced in a dream. For, when awake, man experiences the form of his organs at most by studying scientific anatomy and physiology. That, however, is not a real experience; it is merely looking at them externally, as one looks at stones and plants. So, we may ignore it and say that, in the ordinary consciousness of daily life, man experiences very little, or nothing at all, of his internal organism. The second kind of dream, however, puts this before him in pictures, although in transformed pictures.

"Now, if we study a man's life, we find that it is governed by his ego—more or less, according to his strength of will and character. But the activity of the ego within human life very strongly resembles the first kind of dream-experience. Just try to examine closely whether a person's dreams are such that in them his experiences are greatly, violently altered. In anyone who has such dreams you will find a man of strong will-nature. On the other hand, a man who dreams his life almost as it actually is, not altering it in his dreams, will be found to be a man of weak will.

"Thus, you see the action of the ego within a man's life expressed in the way he shapes his dreams. Such knowledge shows us that we have to relate dreams of the first kind to the human ego. Now we learnt in the last lectures that the ego and astral body are outside the physical and etheric bodies in sleep. Remembering this, we shall not be surprised to learn that Spiritual Science shows us that the ego then takes hold of the pictures of waking life—those pictures that it otherwise takes hold of in ordinary reality through the physical and etheric bodies. The first kind of dream is an activity of the ego outside the physical and etheric bodies.

"What then is the second kind of dream? Of course, it too must have something to do with what is outside the physical and etheric bodies during sleep. It cannot be the ego, for this knows nothing of the symbolic organ-forms presented by the dream. One is forced to see that it is the astral body of man that, in sleep, shapes these symbolic pictures of the inner organs, as the ego the pictures of external experience. Thus, the two kinds of dreams point to the activity of the ego and astral body between falling asleep and waking up.

"We can go further. We have seen what a weak man and what a strong man does in his dreams; we have seen that the weak man dreams of things almost exactly as he experienced them, while the strong man transforms and re-arranges them, coloring them by his own character. Pursuing this to the end, we can compare our result with a man's behavior in waking life. We then discover the following intensely interesting fact. Let a man tell you his dreams; notice how one dream-picture is linked to another; study the configuration of his dreams. Then, having formed an idea of the way he dreams, look at the man himself. Stimulated by the idea you have formed of his dream-life; you will be able to form a good picture of the way he acts in life. This leads us to remarkable secrets of human nature. If you study a man as he acts in life and learn to know his individual character, you will find that only a part of his actions proceeds from his own being, from his ego. If all depended on the ego, a man would really do what he dreams; the violent character would be as violent in life as in his dreams, while one who leaves his life almost unchanged in his dreams, would hold aloof from life at all points, let it take its course, let things happen, shaping his life as little as he shapes his dreams.

"And what a man does over and above this—how does that happen? My dear friends, we can very well say that it is done by God, by the spiritual beings of the world. All that man does, he does not do himself. In fact, he does just as much as he actually dreams; the rest is done through him and to him. Only, in ordinary life we do not train ourselves to observe these things; otherwise, we would discover that we only actively participate in the deeds of life as much as we actively participate in our dreams. The world hinders the violent man from being as violent in life as in dreams; in the weak man instincts are working, and once more life itself adds that which happens through him, and of which he would not dream.

"It is interesting to observe a man in some action of his life and to ask: what comes from him, and what from the world? From him proceeds just as much as he can dream, no more, no less. The world adds something in the case of a weak man and subtracts something in the case of a violent man. Seen in this light, dreams become extraordinarily interesting and give us deep insight into the being of man.

"Through dreams he receives reminiscences of what he has experienced externally since descending to Earth for his present life. 'Imagination' gives us pictures which, in the way they are experienced, can be very like dream-pictures; but they contain, not reminiscences of this earthly life, but of what preceded it. It is quite ridiculous for people who do not know Spiritual Science to say that imaginations may be dreams too. They ought only to consider what it is that we 'dream of' in imaginations. We do not dream of what the senses offer; the content represents man's being before he was endowed with senses. Imagination leads man to a new world.

"When we look into man's inner life we receive the impression that certain symbolic pictures, whether they arise through imagination or in dreams [of the second kind], refer to what is within man, man's internal organization; on the other hand, the imaginations which refer to outer experiences are connected, neither with man's internal organization nor with outer life—*but with experiences of his pre-earthly state.* Beside these imaginations one can only place dream experiences of the first kind, those relating to external experiences of earthly life; but there is no inner connection here between these imaginations and these dreams. Such a connection only exists for dreams of the second kind.

"In such a radical case as this it is especially interesting to observe the dream-life. This differs from the dream-life of our ordinary contemporaries; it is much more interesting, but of course this has its reverse side. Still, objectively considered, illness is more interesting than health; from the subjective side; i.e.. for the person concerned, as well as from the point-of-view of ordinary life, it is another matter. For a knowledge of the human being the dream-life of such a patient is really much more interesting than the dream-life of an ordinary contemporary.

"In such a case, you actually see a kind of connection between the ego and the whole dream-world; one might say, it is almost tangible. And we are led to ask the following questions: What is the relation of the dream pictures that refer to internal organs, to the imaginations that also refer to internal organs?

"Well, viewed 'externally', the pictures of man's inner organization that are given in imagination, point to what was within man before he had his earthly body, before he was on the Earth; the dream-pictures arise when once he is here. The imaginations point to the past, the dream-pictures to the present. But though an ordinary dream-picture that refers to an internal organ would correspond to a caricature of that organ, while the imagination would correspond to the perfect organ, nevertheless the caricature has the inherent possibility of growing into a perfect organ."

An Esoteric Cosmology, Lecture XII, The Devachanic World (Heaven) II, June 8, 1906, Paris, GA 94

"At the first stage of clairvoyance, greater order enters into dreams; man sees marvelous forms and hears words that are pregnant with meaning. It becomes more and more possible to decipher the meaning of dreams and to relate them to actuality. We may dream, for example, that a friend's house is on fire and then hear that he is ill. The first faint glimpses of Devachan [Heaven] give the impression of a sky streaked with clouds which gradually turn into living forms.

"At the second stage of clairvoyance, dreams become precise and clear. The geometrical and symbolic figures employed as the sacred signs of the great religions are, properly speaking, the language of the creative Word, the living hieroglyphs of cosmic speech. Among such symbols are: the cross, the sign of life; the pentagram or five-pointed star, the sign of sound or Word; the hexagram or six-pointed star (two interlaced triangles) the sign of the macrocosm reflected in the microcosm, and so forth. At the second stage of clairvoyance, these signs—which we today delineate in abstract lines—appear full of color, life and radiance on a background of light. They are not, as yet, the garment of living beings; but they indicate, so to say, the norms and laws of creation. These signs were the basis of the animal forms chosen by the earliest Initiates to express the passage of the Sun through the zodiacal constellations. The Initiates translated their visions into such signs and symbols. The most ancient characters employed in Sanskrit, Egyptian, Greek, and Runic scripts—every letter of which has ideographic meaning—were the expressions of heavenly ciphers.

"In dreams, man beholds his own bodily form from without. He sees his body stretched on the couch but merely as an empty sheath. Around this empty form shines a radiant, ovoid form—the astral body. It has the appearance of an aura from which the body has been eliminated. The body itself seems like a hollow, empty mold. It is a vision where everything is reversed as in a photographic negative. The soul of crystal, plant, and animal is seen as a kind of radiation, whereas the physical substance appears as an empty sheath.

"To attain the third stage of Devachan [Heaven], thought must be freed from bondage to the things of the physical world. Man can then live consciously in the world of thought, quite independently of the actual content of thought. The pupil must experience the function of pure intellect, apart from its content. A new world will then be revealed. To the perception of the 'continents' and 'waters' of Devachan (the astral soul of things and the streaming currents of life) will be added the perception of its 'air' or 'atmosphere.' This atmosphere is altogether different from our own; its substance is living, sonorous, sensitive. Waves, gleams of light and sounds arise in response to our gestures, acts and thoughts. Everything that happens on Earth reverberates in colors, light, and sound. Whether it be in sleep or after death, the echoes of Earth can be experienced in these 'airs' of Devachan."

Thus, we have heard about the world of spirit where dreams are as real as physical objects are in the material world and different stages of sleep lead humans over into the realms of heaven (Devachan). Dr. Steiner has graciously laid out in his works a topology of the dreamscapes we encounter in sleep and explained their meaning and purpose. He has walked us through the after-life spheres of morality, much life the spirit of Beatric in *The Divine Comedy* (c. 1321 AD) leading Dante through the spheres of heaven. Although, only Steiner explains the levels of heaven and correlates them to our personal self-development of thinking, feeling, and willing that can turn into higher stages of Moral Imagination, Moral Inspiration, and Moral Intuition. Looking through the eyes of Steiner's clairvoyance we can imagine the realms of Angels, Archangels, and even Archi (Time Spirits) Time Spirits who permeate our thinking, feeling, and willing throughout the day, as well as during sleep and after death. Through a deep study of Steiner's *"Book of the Dead"* and his many profound and comprehensive indications about sleep, dreams, and death, the aspirant of Spiritual Science can approach the invisible realms with confidence that innumerable spiritual beings stand ready, at all times, to help serve as veritable midwives for our birth into the Divine World of the Spiritual Hierarchies. While sleep, the "little sister of death", is re-envisioned as a nightly practice to help prepare us for death and our re-birth into the Spiritual World.

Whether you take up the suggested practice of reading Steiner's *"Book of the Dead"* to your love ones after they pass over the threshold into the spiritual world, or you simply read and study the content to advance your own understanding of the question of life after death, Dr Steiner's work is the most direct way to map out the path that we all are taking back to the 'home' we lived in before we came down to our earthly birth. The pre-birth realm and the after-death realm are the same world as seen from two different perspectives. Once a full cosmological understanding of the Kingdoms of Nature and the Kingdoms of the Spiritual Hierarchies is attained through Spiritual Science, the aspirant realizes that the entire Cosmos is contained within their personal "I Am."

> "I have said, Ye are gods; and all of you are children of the most High."
> *Psalm* (82:6)

This "god in the becoming" reigns as the monarch of their own Sun, the human heart; which is the door to the spiritual world whether the aspirant is entering sleep or is taking the "long sleep" of death. Either way, the same beings are there to assist the process and guide the aspirant lovingly through a reciprocal nourishing communion, a two-way communication through the Language of the Spirit, and by giving the aspirant the blessed gifts of the night that arrive as Moral Imagination, Moral Inspiration, and Moral Intuition. These gifts of the spirit are spiritual treasures of the invisible night that feed and nourish and enlighten our day.

Awaken dear aspirant to the promptings of the Holy Spirit and lift the veil of Isis-Sophia to find true life and wisdom through freedom and love; whether it be in sleep or through death and rebirth. For the Spiritual World awaits you with open arms if you can cross the threshold in good conscience and with an awakened consciousness. Therefore, trim your "candle of vision" and be ye ever mindful of the song that dwells within your heart-of-hearts; for there is nothing greater than awaiting the groom who comes in the dark of night to wed the awakened, pure Virgin Soul in the heavenly marriage of the Bride to the Lamb the marriage of Sophia to Christ.

> "Behold, I send you forth as sheep in the midst of wolves: be ye therefore wise as serpents, and harmless as doves."
> *Matthew* (10:16)

Michaelic Verse For Our Times
by Rudolf Steiner

We must eradicate from the soul all fear and terror of
what comes toward us out of the future.
We must acquire serenity in all feelings and sensations about the future.
We must look forward with absolute equanimity to all that may come,
and we must think only that whatever comes is given to us
by a world direction full of wisdom.
This is what we have to learn in our times.
To live out of pure trust in the ever present help of the spiritual world.
Surely nothing else will do, if our courage is not to fail us.
Let us properly discipline our will, and let us seek
the inner awakening every morning and every evening.

BIBLIOGRAPHY

- Andreæ, Johann Valentin. *Reipublicæ Christianopolitanæ descriptio*. Argentorati: Sumptibus hæredum Lazari Zetzneri, Strasbourg, 1619.

- Andreæ, Johann Valentin. *Johann Valentin Andreae's Christianopolis; an ideal state of the seventeenth century.* translated from the Latin of Johann Valentin Andreae with an historical introduction. by Felix Emil Held. The Graduate School of the University of Illinois, Urbana- Champaign, 1916.

- Arnold, Edwin Sir. *The Light of Asia, or The Great Renunciation (Mahâbhinishkramana): Being the Life and Teaching Gautama, Prince of India and Founder of Buddhism (As Told in Verse by an Indian Buddhist)*. Kegan Paul, Trench, Trübner & Co., London, 1879.

- Avari, Burjor. *India: The Ancient Past: A History of the Indian Sub-Continent*. Routledge, New Edition, 2007.

- Barnwell, John. *The Arcana of the Grail Angel: The Spiritual Science of the Holy Blood and of the Holy Grail*. Verticordia Press, Bloomfield Hills, 1999.

- Barnwell, John. *The Arcana of Light on the Path: The Star Wisdom of the Tarot and Light on the Path*. Verticordia Press, Bloomfield Hills, 1999.

- Blavatsky, H. P. (Helena Petrovna). *Isis Unveiled: A Master-Key to the Mysteries of Ancient and Modern Science and Theology*. J. W. Bouton. New York, 1878.

- Blavatsky, H. P. (Helena Petrovna). *The Key to Theosophy: Being a Clear Exposition, in the Form of Question and Answer, of the Ethics, Science and Philosophy for the Study of Which the Theosophical Society Has Been Founded.* The Theosophical Publishing Company, Ltd. London, 1889.

- Blavatsky, H. P. (Helena Petrovna). *The Secret Doctrine: The Synthesis of Science, Religion and Philosophy.* The Theosophical Publishing Company, Ltd. London, 1888.

- Blavatsky, H. P. (Helena Petrovna). *The Voice of Silence: Being Extracts from the Book of the Golden Precepts.* Theosophical University Press, 1992.

- Bockemuhl, Jochen. *Toward a Phenomenology of the Etheric World: Investigations into the Life of Nature and Man.* Anthroposophic Press, Spring Valley, N. Y., 1977.

- Campanella, Tommaso. *The City of the Sun.* The ProjectGutenberg Ebook, David Widger, 2013.

- Colum, Padriac. *Orpheus: Myths of the World.* Floris Books. Colum, Padriac. The Children's Homer. MacMillan Co., 1946.

- Colum, Padriac. *The Tales of Ancient Egypt.* Henry Walck Incorporated, New York,1968.

- Crawford, John Martin. *The Kalevala: The Epic Poem of Finland.* John B. Alden, New York, 1888.

- Gabriel, Douglas. *The Eternal Curriculum for Wisdom Children: Intuitive Learning and the Etheric Body.* Our Spirit, Northville, 2017.

- Gabriel, Tyla. *The Gospel of Sophia: The Biographies of the Divine Feminine Trinity,* Volume, Our Spirit, Northville, 2014.

Bibliography

- Gabriel, Tyla. *The Gospel of Sophia: A Modern Path of Initiation,* Volume 2. Our Spirit, Northville, 2015.

- Gabriel, Tyla and Douglas. *The Gospel of Sophia: Sophia Christos Initiation,* Volume 3. Our Spirit, Northville, 2016.

- Gabriel, Douglas. *The Spirit of Childhood.* Trinosophia Press, Berkley, 1993.

- Gabriel, Douglas. *The Eternal Ethers: A Theory of Everything.* Our Spirit, Northville, 2018.

- Gabriel, Douglas. *Goddess Meditations.* Trinosophia Press, Berkley, 1994.

- Gebser, Jean. *The Ever Present Origin.* Ohio University Press, 1991.

- Green, Roger Lancelyn & Heather Copley. *Tales of Ancient Egypt.* Puffin Books, New York, 1980.

- Harrison, C. G. *The Transcendental Universe; Six Lectures on Occult Science, Theosophy, and the Catholic Faith.* George Redway, London 1893.

- Harrison, C. G. *The Transcendental Universe; Six Lectures on Occult Science, Theosophy, and the Catholic Faith.* Delivered Before the Berean Society, edited with an introduction by Christopher Bamford. Lindesfarne Press, Hudson, 1993.

- Hamilton, Edith. *Mythology.* Little Brown And Co., Boston, 1942.

- Harrer, Dorothy. *Chapters from Ancient History.* Waldorf Publications, Chatham, 2016.

- Hazeltine, Alice Isabel. *Hero Tales from Many Lands.* Abingdon Press, New York, 1961.

- Heidel, Alexander. *The Babylonian Genesis: The Story of Creation.* University of Chicago Press, Chicago, 1942.

- Hiebel, Frederick. *The Gospel of Hellas.* Anthroposophic Press, New York, 1949.

- Jocelyn, Beredene. *Citizens of the Cosmos: Life's Unfolding from Conception through Death to Rebirth.* Continuum, New York, 1981.

- König, Karl. *Earth and Man.* Bio-Dynamic Literature, Wyoming, Rhode Island, 1982.

- Kovacs, Charles. *Ancient Mythologies and History.* Resource Books, Scotland, 1991.

- Kovacs, Charles. *Greek Mythology and History.* Resource Books, Scotland, 1991.

- Landscheidt, Theodor. *Sun-Earth-Man a Mesh of Cosmic Oscillations: How Planets Regulate Solar Eruptions, Geomagnetic Storms, Conditions of Life, and Economic Cycles.* Urania Trust, London, 1989.

- Laszlo, Ervin and Kingsley, Dennis L. *Dawn of the Akashic Age: New Consciousness, Quantum Resonance, and the Future of the World.* Inner Traditions, Rochester Vermont, 2013

- Plato. *The Republic.* Dover Thrift Editions, 2000.

- Sister Nivedita (Margaret E. Noble) & Coomaraswamy, Ananda K.. *Myths of the Hindus and Buddhists.* Henry Holt, New York 1914.

- Steiner, Rudolf. *Ancient Myths: Their Meaning and Connection with Evolution.* Steiner Book Center, 1971.

- Steiner, Rudolf. *Christ and the Spiritual World: The Search for the Holy Grail.* Rudolf Steiner Press, London, 1963.

Bibliography

- Steiner, Rudolf. *Foundations of Esotericism*. Rudolf Steiner Press, London, 1983.

- Steiner, Rudolf. *Isis Mary Sophia: Her Mission and Ours*. Steiner Books, 2003.

- Steiner, Rudolf. *Man as a Being of Sense and Perception*. Steiner Book Center, Vancouver, 1981.

- Steiner, Rudolf. *Man as Symphony of the Creative Word*. Rudolf Steiner Publishing, London, 1978.

- Steiner, Rudolf. *Occult Science*. Anthroposophic Press, NY, 1972.

- Steiner, Rudolf. *Rosicrucian Esotericism*. Anthroposophic Press, NY, 1978.

- Steiner, Rudolf. *Rosicrucian Wisdom: An Introduction*. Rudolf Steiner Press, London, 2000. GA 425

- Steiner, Rudolf. *The Bridge between Universal Spirituality and the Physical Constitution of Man*. Anthroposophic Press, NY, 1958.

- Steiner, Rudolf. *The Evolution of Consciousness*. Rudolf Steiner Press, London, 1926.

- Steiner, Rudolf. *The Goddess from Natura to the Divine Sophia*. Sophia Books, 2001.

- Steiner, Rudolf. *The Holy Grail: from the Works of Rudolf Steiner*. Compiled by Steven Roboz, Steiner Book Center, North Vancouver, 1984.

- Steiner, Rudolf. *The Influence of Spiritual Beings Upon Man*. Anthroposophic Press, NY, 1971.

- Steiner, Rudolf. *The Reappearance of Christ in the Etheric*. Anthroposophic Press, NY, 1983.

- Steiner, Rudolf. *The Risen Christ and the Etheric Christ*. Rudolf Steiner Press, London, 1969.

- Steiner, Rudolf. *The Search for the New Isis the Divine Sophia*. Mercury Press, N.Y., 1983.

- Steiner, Rudolf. *The Spiritual Hierarchies and the Physical World*. Anthroposophic Press, N.Y., 1996.

- Steiner, Rudolf. *The Tree of Life and the Tree of Knowledge*. Mercury Press, NY, 2006.

- Steiner, Rudolf. *The True Nature of the Second Coming*. Rudolf Steiner Press, London, 1971.

- Steiner, Rudolf. *Theosophy*. Anthroposophic Press. New York, 1986.

- Steiner, Rudolf. *Wonders of the World, Ordeals of the Soul, Revelations of the Spirit*. Rudolf Steiner Press, London, 1963.

- Steiner, Rudolf. *World History in Light of Anthroposophy*. Rudolf Steiner Press, London, 1977.

- Tappan, Eva March. *The Story of the Greek People*. Houghton Mifflin Co., Boston 1908.

- van Bemmelen, D. J. *Zarathustra: The First Prophet of Christ*, 2 Vols. Uitgeverij Vrij Geestesleven, The Netherlands, 1968.

- Watson, Jane Werner (Vālmīki). *Rama of the Golden Age: An Epic of India*. Garrard Pub., Champaign.

ABOUT DR. RUDOLF STEINER

Rudolf Steiner was born on the 27th of February 1861 in Kraljevec in the former Kingdom of Hungary and now Croatia. He studied at the College of Technology in Vienna and obtained his doctorate at the University of Rostock with a dissertation on Theory of Knowledge which concluded with the sentence: "The most important problem of human thinking is this: to understand the human being as a free personality, whose very foundation is himself."

He exchanged views widely with the personalities involved in cultural life and arts of his time. However, unlike them, he experienced the spiritual realm as the other side of reality. He gained access through exploration of consciousness using the same method as the natural scientist uses for the visible world in his external research. This widened perspective enabled him to give significant impulses in many areas such as art, pedagogy, curative education, medicine, agriculture, architecture, economics, and social sciences, aiming towards the spiritual renewal of civilization.

He gave his movement the name of "Anthroposophy" (the wisdom of humanity) after separating from the German section of the Theosophical Society, where he had acted as a general secretary. He then founded the Anthroposophical Society in 1913 which formed its center with the construction of the First Goetheanum in Dornach, Switzerland. Rudolf Steiner died on 30th March 1925 in Dornach. His literary work is made up of numerous books, transcripts and approximately 6000 lectures which have for the most part been edited and published in the Complete Works Edition.

Steiner's basic books, which were previously a prerequisite to gaining access to his lectures, are: *Theosophy, The Philosophy of Freedom, How to Know Higher Worlds, Christianity as a Mystical Fact,* and *Occult Science.*

ABOUT THE AUTHOR, DR. DOUGLAS GABRIEL

Dr. Gabriel is a retired superintendent of schools and professor of education who has worked with schools and organizations throughout the world. He has authored many books ranging from teacher training manuals to philosophical/spiritual works on the nature of the divine feminine.

He was a Waldorf class teacher and administrator at the Detroit Waldorf School and taught courses at Mercy College, the University of Detroit, and Wayne State University for decades. He then became the Headmaster of a Waldorf School in Hawaii and taught at the University of Hawaii, Hilo. He was a leader in the development of charter schools in Michigan and helped found the first Waldorf School in the Detroit Public School system and the first charter Waldorf School in Michigan.

Gabriel received his first degree in religious formation at the same time as an associate degree in computer science in 1972. This odd mixture of technology and religion continued throughout his life. He was drafted into and served in the Army Security Agency (NSA) where he was a cryptologist and systems analyst in signal intelligence, earning him a degree in signal broadcasting. After military service, he entered the Catholic Church again as a Trappist monk and later as a Jesuit priest where he earned PhD's in philosophy and comparative religion, and a Doctor of Divinity. He came to Detroit and earned a BA in anthroposophical studies and history and a MA in school administration. Gabriel left the priesthood and became a Waldorf class teacher and administrator in Detroit and later in Hilo, Hawaii.

Douglas has been a sought-after lecturer and consultant to schools and businesses throughout the world and in 1982 he founded the Waldorf Educational Foundation that provides funding for the publication of educational books. He has raised a great deal of money for Waldorf schools and institutions that continue to develop the teachings of Dr. Rudolf Steiner. Douglas is now retired but continues to write a variety of books including a novel and a science fiction thriller. He has four children, who keep him busy and active and a wife who is always striving towards the spirit through creating an "art of life." She is the author of the Gospel of Sophia trilogy.

The Gabriels' articles, blogs, and videos can currently be found at:

OurSpirit.com,
Neoanthroposphy.com,
GospelofSophia.com,
EternalCurriculum.com

TRANSLATOR'S NOTE

The Rudolf Steiner quotes in this book can be found, in most cases, in their full-length and in context, through the Rudolf Steiner Archives by an Internet search of the references provided. We present the quoted selections of Steiner from a free rendered translation of the original while utilizing comparisons of numerous German to English translations that are available from a variety of publishers and other sources. In some cases, the quoted selections may be condensed and partially summarized using the same, or similar in meaning, words found in the original. Brackets are used to insert [from the author] clarifying details or anthroposophical nomenclature and spiritual scientific terms.

We chose to use GA (Gesamtausgabe—collected edition) numbers to reference Steiner's works instead of CW (Collected Works), which is often used in English editions. Some books in the series, *From the Works of Rudolf Steiner*, have consciously chosen to use a predominance of Steiner quotes to drive the presentation of the themes rather than personal remarks and commentary.

We feel that Steiner's descriptions should not be truncated but need to be translated into an easily read format for the English-speaking reader, especially for those new to Anthroposophy. We recommend that serious aspirants read the entire lecture, or chapter, from which the Steiner quotation was taken, because nothing can replace Steiner's original words or the mood in which they were delivered. The style of speaking and writing has changed dramatically over the last century and needs updating in style and presentation to translate into a useful tool for spiritual study in modern times. The series, *From the Works of Rudolf Steiner* intends to present numerous "study guides" for the beginning aspirant, and the initiate, in a format that helps support the spiritual scientific research of the reader.

Made in the USA
Las Vegas, NV
25 March 2025